THE INTENTIONAL TEACHER:
CONTROLLER, MANAGER, HELPER

BASIC CONCEPTS IN EDUCATIONAL PSYCHOLOGY SERIES

Larry R. Goulet, University of Illinois, Series Editor

LANGUAGE, LEARNING, AND COGNITIVE PROCESSES
Francis J. Di Vesta, The Pennsylvania State University

GROWING CHILDREN
Lynn Dorman
Freda Rebelsky, Boston University

INSTRUCTIONAL APPLICATIONS OF BEHAVIOR PRINCIPLES
J. Ronald Gentile, State University of New York at Buffalo
Thomas W. Frazier, Behavioral Technology Consultants
Mary C. Morris, Behavioral Technology Consultants

EVALUATION IN THE SCHOOLS: A HUMAN PROCESS
FOR RENEWAL
John L. Hayman, Jr., University of Alabama
Rodney N. Napier, The Athyn Group, Philadelphia, Pennsylvania

SOCIOCULTURAL ORIGINS OF ACHIEVEMENT
Martin L. Maehr, University of Illinois

THE INTENTIONAL TEACHER: CONTROLLER, MANAGER, HELPER
Robert J. Menges, Northwestern University

LEARNING AND INSTRUCTION
Thomas J. Shuell, State University of New York at Buffalo
Claudia Z. Lee, State University of New York at Buffalo

STANDARDIZED TESTING IN THE SCHOOLS:
USES AND ROLES
James L. Wardrop, University of Illinois

THE INTENTIONAL TEACHER: CONTROLLER, MANAGER, HELPER

ROBERT J. MENGES
Northwestern University

BROOKS/COLE PUBLISHING COMPANY
MONTEREY, CALIFORNIA
A Division of Wadsworth Publishing Company, Inc.

Printed in the United States of America

10 9 8 7 6 5 4 3 2 1

Library of Congress Cataloging in Publication Data

Menges Robert J.
   The intentional teacher.
   (Basic concepts in educational psychology series)
   Bibliography: p. 111.
   Includes index.
   1. Teaching. 2. Classroom management. 3. Behavior modification. I. Title.
   LB1025.2.M445   371:1′02   76-26859
   ISBN 0-8185-0209-6

Manuscript Editor: *Barbara Mountrey*
Production Editor: *Fiorella Ljunggren*
Interior and Cover Design: *Linda Marcetti*

To Gay

SERIES FOREWORD

The present time is an exciting period in the history of education. We are reconceptualizing the nature of formal settings in which teaching and learning take place. In addition, we are developing alternative models for teaching and learning. We have rediscovered the importance of the home, parents, and peers in the educational process. And, we are experiencing rapid change and continual advances in the technology of teaching and in the definition of the goals, objectives, and products of education.

The broad concern with the process of education has created new audiences for education-related courses, a demand for new offerings, and the need for increased flexibility in the format for courses. Furthermore, colleges and schools of education are initiating new courses and curricula that appeal to the broad range of undergraduates and that focus squarely on current and relevant social and educational issues.

The Basic Concepts in Educational Psychology series is designed to provide flexibility for both the instructor and the student. The scope of the series is broad, yet each volume in the series is self-contained and may be used as either a primary or a supplementary text. In addition, the topics for the volumes in the series have been carefully chosen so that several books in the series may be adopted for use in introductory courses or in courses with a more specialized focus. Furthermore, each of the volumes is suitable for use in classes operating on the semester or quarter system, or for modular, in-service training, or workshop modes of instruction.

Larry R. Goulet

PREFACE

Teaching calls for extraordinary energy and skills. Teaching goes on in a variety of settings besides schools, and one reason for writing this book is to describe the teaching/learning process in nonclassroom settings. I analyze voluntary groups such as Alcoholics Anonymous, outdoor education programs such as Outward Bound, and self-control projects done by students as they go about daily tasks. In each of these examples there are teachers and learners, but their goals and relationships differ in ways that deserve the attention of educators.

The Intentional Teacher may be used to introduce the study of teaching and learning to undergraduates preparing for human-service professions. Professional-school students and those who work with learners as youth leaders, religious educators, counselors, school administrators, professors, and social workers also should find this point of view pertinent. Parents are teachers too, and those who hope to be intentional teachers may find some value in these pages as well.

One way of considering the variety of teaching/learning activities is to conceptualize three teacher roles. Depending on objectives and other circumstances, a teacher sometimes assumes the role of controller, sometimes the role of manager, and sometimes the role of helper. These roles are illustrated in Chapter One, and each is described further in a subsequent chapter.

Intentionality is the dimension underlying my conception of teaching. The intentional teacher is one whose actions and intentions are congruent. Such teachers know what they intend and are able to select appropriate means for themselves and for their students to actualize those intentions. My final chapter discusses intentions in some detail and suggests ways teachers might clarify intentions and come closer to achieving them in practice.

As the outline of this book was developing, I benefited from the support of Charles Williams of the Lilly Endowment and from the encouragement of Merton Strommen, Sara Little, Shelby Andress, and

Francis Gamelin, with whom I was engaged in a project for the Youth Research Center in Minneapolis. Bill McGaghie of the University of Illinois and James Kulik of the University of Michigan provided helpful reviews of the manuscript.

I am also grateful to many students who commented on earlier drafts, including students at Northwestern University, Princeton Theological Seminary, and the University of Illinois.

Finally, I appreciate the encouragement of Larry Goulet, the typing of Emily Demme and Kay McCormick, and the efficient work of the Brooks/Cole staff during the final publication process.

Robert J. Menges

CONTENTS

CHAPTER ONE
AN INTRODUCTION TO THE THREE TEACHER ROLES   1

CHAPTER TWO
THE TEACHER AS CONTROLLER   5

Dealing with Misbehavior (or The Taming of the Student)   6
The Experimental Analysis of Behavior   7
    The Behavioral Approach   7
    Twin Oaks: A Community Based on Behavioral Psychology   11
    Some Claims for the Behavioral Approach   13
Objections to the Behavioral Approach   17
    The Philosophical Objections   18
    The Practical Objections   19
    The Empirical Objections   20
Behavioral Self-Modification   23
    Self-Modification Projects for College Students   23
    Some Problems for Research   26
    Self-Modification and Objections to the Behavioral Approach   28
Psychopower and the Teacher as Controller   30
For Further Reading   31

CHAPTER THREE
THE TEACHER AS MANAGER   33

Three Key Management Decisions   34
Mastery Learning   34
    Assumptions about the Learner   37
    Decision Roles   38

xi

Teacher-Learner Contracts   38
   The Interpersonal Dimension of Contracts   39
   Decision Roles   41
Games and Simulations   41
   The Process of Learning from Experience   43
   Decision Roles   44
Total Immersion   44
   Taking the Plunge in Chicago   46
   Taking the Wilderness Solo   47
   Decision Roles   49
Learners as Teachers   49
   Tutoring among Unequals   51
   A Triangle of Outcomes   52
   Decision Roles   53
Learning Networks   53
   Decision Roles   54
Decision Making and the Teacher as Manager   56
For Further Reading   57

CHAPTER FOUR
THE TEACHER AS HELPER   61

The Teacher as Helper: Empathic Communication   64
   Empathic Response   64
   I-Messages   65
   Two Classroom Discussions   66
The Group as Helper   70
   Encounter Groups: Facilitating Personal Growth   72
   Training Groups: Facilitating Professional Growth   76
   Research on Encounter and Training Groups   80
   Mutual-Aid and Self-Help Groups   83
   Effectiveness of Mutual Aid and Self-Help Groups   91
The Helping Role in Teaching and Learning   92
For Further Reading   94

CHAPTER FIVE
THE INTENTIONAL TEACHER   96

Why Do People Do What They Do?   96
The Discrepancy between Intention and Behavior   97
Three Views of Intentions   98
   A View from Psychoanalysis   99

A View from Social Psychology   100
A View from Behavioral Psychology   102
A Program for Increasing Intention-Behavior Congruence   105
Toward More Adequate Intentions   105
Toward More Comprehensive Feedback   107
Intentional Teachers Anonymous   108
For Further Reading   109

REFERENCES   111
AUTHOR INDEX   119
SUBJECT INDEX   123

CHAPTER ONE

AN INTRODUCTION TO THE THREE TEACHER ROLES

In this book we look at teachers, at their relationships with learners, and in particular at three roles teachers may take as they assist learners. These are the roles of controller, of manager, and of helper.

These roles represent three points of focus for a teacher's efforts. In the role of controller, a teacher aims at changes in very specific learner behaviors, behaviors that can be observed. In the role of manager, a teacher seeks to enhance subject-matter learning by arranging an appropriate setting for learning. In the role of helper, a teacher promotes the development and expression of the learner's feelings and emotions.

These roles are useful to keep in mind in virtually any teaching/learning situation and with learners of virtually any age as learning goals and strategies are selected. The particular focus of each role is illustrated below in three teaching/learning situations. The first involves a fifth-grade class, the second involves a conservation club, and the third involves a religious-education group.

Social Studies Class

A fifth-grade social studies class is studying the electoral process. Several students have been consistently disruptive during time allocated for quiet study. They disturb others who are working and never complete their own assignments, no matter how much they are scolded. The teacher decides that for each ten-minute period of uninterrupted work, students will receive one unit of credit toward a coming field trip. The trip can be taken only if enough credits are accumulated. As a result, the disruptive students become much more attentive, and, as the classroom atmosphere improves, other students begin to compliment them. The teacher has acted as *controller* by establishing positive consequences for productive classroom behavior.

In studying the electoral college, students in the class find textbook descriptions difficult to understand. The teacher plans a game that recreates actions of the electorate, of candidates, and of the electoral college during a presidential election year. Students are enthusiastic about the game, particularly those who take major roles in it, and their class discussions seem to be better informed. The teacher has acted as *manager* by selecting a strategy in which students can become involved with the topic more personally than they could when merely reading a text. The students' learning has increased as a result of this management decision by the teacher.

Several of the students have raised thoughtful questions about the class. They seriously wonder what their social studies work can be good for. The teacher knows that pronouncements about good citizenship will not satisfy them; besides, the teacher has personal reservations about parts of the curriculum. During a classroom discussion the teacher reveals some of these reservations and encourages students to speak freely about their concerns. The discussion settles nothing, of course, yet several students appear to be more serious and curious in their activities during the next few weeks. The teacher acted as *helper* by eliciting the expression of feelings and by indicating that even negative feelings about the class are acceptable.

Outdoor Conservation Club

College students in an outdoor conservation club are preparing for a "survival" trip. During their physical-conditioning sessions, the leader notices that jogging is popular, but arm and shoulder exercises are being neglected. Since every member has a quota of exercise points to earn at each session, the leader modifies the scoring so that push-ups increase and jogging decreases in point value. Soon members have shifted their activities to a more appropriate balance between the two types of exercises. The leader has *controlled* members' behavior, not directly—a command to do more push-ups would be an attempt at direct control—but indirectly, by making the desired behavior more attractive.

During the coming trip, members will sometimes travel together and sometimes be alone. In order to help members anticipate the loneliness of their trip, the leader schedules a "solo" for each member. A 30-hour period is spent alone under conditions like those to be encountered. The leader cannot know precisely what events will occur during the solo but assumes that the environment will serve as an effective teacher. As *manager,* the leader has devised a learning activity much more powerful than group discussion or formal study.

Morale in the group is sometimes poor, a fact that bodes ill for their proximity and interdependence on the trip. The leader's pep talks increase in passion, but morale seems to sink even lower. In conversations with each member, the leader learns that the members are bothered by apparent rivalries within the group and that some of them even perceive the leader to be playing favorites. Subsequently, the leader takes care to avoid any suggestion of favoritism and encourages discussion of this issue during group meetings. The leader has acted as *helper* by legitimizing and encouraging expression of personal feelings within the group.

Religious-Study Group

A religious-study group of high school students is studying issues of ethics in the medical profession. The project started slowly, because students did not know the names of medical specialties and other significant terminology. They decided to let no one begin the more interesting parts of the project until all had learned these terms. The advisor suggested that they divide into subgroups and earn points for each bit of completed memorization. Groups sometimes study between meetings to prepare for the review quiz that all must pass. The students have moved toward *self-control* by adopting the method of rewarding small bits of progress on an important, but not particularly pleasant, task.

In order to learn firsthand about the issues that arise in day-to-day medical practice, each student becomes the "shadow" of a doctor. The student follows the doctor everywhere—so long as no one's privacy is violated—taking special note of all incidents that have ethical implications. The advisor has acted as *manager* by arranging opportunities to observe directly the issues that the group seeks to understand.

Later the group meets to share their observations. During these discussions, members become involved in heated arguments, some siding with doctors and some always siding with patients. The advisor conducts several role-playing exercises on the topic of malpractice. In these exercises students sometimes take the role of doctor and sometimes take the role of patient. After a time, students seem to gain some empathy for both points of view. The advisor has acted as *helper* by assisting students to identify emotionally with persons whose views they previously rejected.

The thesis of this book is that the work of most teachers can be usefully conceptualized in terms of the roles just illustrated. There are some situations in which the teacher intends to act as controller by affecting very specific learner behaviors. In other situations the teacher intends to be a manager, choosing the proper balance between teacher responsibilities and student responsibilities in designing appropriate learning activities. At still other times the teacher intends to be a helper, facilitating the expression and understanding of feelings. Each of these roles is elaborated in a subsequent chapter.

Of course not all intentions are carried out in behavior. Reducing the discrepancy between intention and behavior is another important subject of this book and is discussed in Chapter Five. The intentional teacher—one whose intentions and behaviors are congruent—possesses the skills to be controller or manager or helper. The intentional teacher also has the wisdom to decide which role is appropriate in a particular teaching/learning situation. This wisdom is another expression of the teacher's intentionality.

In these chapters I typically use the terms *teacher* and *learner* (sometimes *student* or, for younger children, *pupil*). My preference is for the general term *learner,* because I do not wish to speak only about conventional school settings. I believe these roles are appropriate for teachers of children in schools, to be sure, but also for many other settings: for coaches on the practice field, for physical therapists with patients, for professors in colleges, for directors of volunteer service agencies. Indeed, all those who work to bring about learning should be able to identify with these roles.

The intentional teacher is the teacher who has a great variety of skills and who has the metaskill to choose appropriately among them. The concept of the intentional teacher is applicable to anyone who assists others to learn.

CHAPTER
TWO
THE TEACHER
AS CONTROLLER

The traditional view of education, a view that still prevails, holds that learners must submit themselves to teachers. Learners are by definition persons lacking in experience, whereas teachers are persons of greater knowledge, wisdom, and experience. When education is successful, learners become more like their teachers in knowledge and possibly in wisdom. Ultimately, learners generate their own experience and may eventually surpass their teachers.

The troublesome aspect of this view, in my opinion, is the notion that learners "submit themselves." Teachers may use this view to insist on uniformity from students. Schools and communities, too, may demand strict conformity to certain patterns of student movement, noise level, and appearance. In such situations teachers' authority is not to be questioned; learners are evaluated on the basis of obedience as well as learning. The assumption is that without such constraints on students, learning will not occur.

Surveys of public attitudes show that this concern for standards of student behavior is widespread. Since 1969, Gallup International has conducted annual national polls about the public schools. Lack of discipline has been rated the number one problem nearly every year. In a recent survey three of the top four problems had to do with student behavior: lack of discipline, integration/segregation problems, and use of drugs. (The fourth concerned the financing of education.) Students rank the same problems as important. And student discipline is well known to be a perennial concern of teachers (Gallup, 1974).

Some educators have suggested institutional alternatives to this prevailing view. Alternative schools and open classrooms have been suggested as ways of reducing the controls required in a system of compulsory schooling. But since the controlled system is what our society apparently prefers, I shall discuss it rather than some alternative.

My aim in this chapter is first to examine how teachers have customarily attempted to control student behavior in order to promote

5

learning and then to consider in some detail the contributions of the "experimental analysis of behavior" in dealing with behavior problems. I shall discuss objections to the behavioral approach, as well, and suggest that its ultimate use in education is not to enable teachers to effectively control the behavior of learners, but to enable teachers to assist learners to gain control over their own behavior.

DEALING WITH MISBEHAVIOR
(OR, THE TAMING OF THE STUDENT)

At its most extreme, the insistence that students submit themselves to teachers implies that students are primitive creatures who must be tamed. They are seen as young and immature; lacking civilized, socialized skills; undisciplined and irresponsible (Willower, Eidell, & Hoy, 1973). A defense of corporal punishment follows from this view: corporal punishment forces students to cease misbehaving, and fear of severe punishment prevents the recurrence of misbehavior.

Viewing the student as a creature to be tamed also implies a moral judgment. Students are seen as unworthy, or at least as obliged to prove their worth. Teachers, by definition morally superior, are then affronted if students misbehave. Misbehavior is interpreted as an expression of dislike for the teacher, who naturally responds by a reassertion of authority. Both students and teachers are caught in relationships of escalating hostility.

Most teachers are well intentioned and do not wish to control students by threat of punishment. Yet research shows that most of the time teachers are more disapproving than approving. Consider one dramatic (but typical) finding: only 8% of teachers use approval, rather than disapproval, in more than half of their classroom interactions with students (Madsen & Madsen, 1974). Another study of 104 teachers found that in every grade after the second, the teacher gave more disapproval than approval to pupils (White, 1975).

Many punishments are available to teachers. Besides corporal punishment and direct verbal or nonverbal disapproval, there are ridicule, extra work, social ostracism, forced silence, extra school time, suspension, and expulsion. Skinner (1968, Chapter 5) notes that threat of aversive (punishing) consequences is what holds school together. Does schoolwork cease when the teacher is not present to threaten? Is dismissal when class ends rewarding (an escape from threat)? Are well-behaved students excused from assignments?

How do students describe what happens when they do good schoolwork? Are they concerned with the rewards that come from learning, or do they find satisfaction in having avoided the aversive consequences of *not* learning?

Teacher dependence on punishment and on the threat of punishment is seen by Skinner and others as responsible for a host of problems. Students are late to school or skip school entirely. In school, they are restless, inattentive, and disruptive (although out of school they may show long periods of absorbed attention), or they withdraw psychologically much of the time. Teachers learn to keep their distance psychologically from students and to "get tough." School facilities are targets of vandalism. All of these are predictable side effects of aversive control.

If we agree that aversive control is not working, what alternative is there? If we agree that a moralistic approach to students is inadequate, where do we seek the causes of behavior and misbehavior? One alternative approach follows.

THE EXPERIMENTAL ANALYSIS OF BEHAVIOR

The careful analysis of what people do in order to understand the causes of their actions is termed the "experimental analysis of behavior." A child (or a classroom) is observed and a record is made of the actions observed. If possible, the child is studied in a controlled environment, perhaps a laboratory, where a single variable may be changed in order to determine how that variable modifies the child's behavior. Hundreds of such careful studies have been done, and this work constitutes what B. F. Skinner and others call the behavioral approach.

THE BEHAVIORAL APPROACH

In discussing teaching and learning, Skinner asserts that there are three major variables relevant to the learning process: "(1) an occasion upon which behavior occurs, (2) the behavior itself, and (3) the consequences of the behavior" (Skinner, 1968, p. 4). These variables deserve illustration.

First, let us use these variables to analyze a naturally occurring learning situation, a boy's beginning to walk. Variable 1: His eyes fix on a favorite toy across the room (occasion). Variable 2: He moves in the direction of the toy, arms poised both to break a fall and to grasp the toy (behavior). Variable 3: His movements result in consequences which are pleasant, holding the toy, or aversive, violent contact with the floor (consequences). In this natural example, although learning may occur, teaching does not. "The school of experience is no school at all, not because no one learns in it, but because no one teaches. Teaching is the expediting of learning; a person who is taught learns more quickly than one who is not" (Skinner, 1968, p. 5).

Next let us analyze a situation in which teaching as well as learning occurs. A young girl learns to write the alphabet using a workbook. Variable 1: The teacher requests that she work on a particular page (occasion). Variable 2: She completes special letters on the page that gradually "vanish" until she is writing the entire letter from memory (behavior). Variable 3: Her special pen makes a yellow mark on the chemically treated paper when she fails to follow the outline of an acceptable letter and a gray mark when the letter is acceptable (consequences). (The child is first taught that gray is desirable.) These immediately available consequences will enhance learning, according to Skinner (1968). Because they are a deliberately arranged part of the situation, the child truly has been taught.

What is the particular contribution of the experimental analysis of behavior? The traditional approach has attempted to control behavior (variable number 2) directly, primarily through threat of punishment. The behavioral approach deals indirectly with behavior by controlling its antecedents (variable 1) or its consequences (variable 3) or both.

The control of antecedents. In Homer's *Odyssey*, Ulysses avoided shipwreck by a clever application of antecedent control. The Sirens had lured ships to destruction on the rocky shores as crews strained toward the sound of the Sirens' song. Ulysses knew that the crew should not be permitted to hear the songs, so he had the men fill their ears with wax. He wished to hear the songs himself but feared he would then change the ship's course. So he had his men bind him to the mast during the time he could hear the music. Ulysses altered the occasion upon which the behavior in question occurred.

Similarly a teacher may identify circumstances that regularly precede disruptive behavior and, by avoiding those circumstances, may avoid the disruption. More desirably, the teacher may be able to create situations that encourage concentration and participation and may thereby increase productive student behavior. For example, different sections of the classroom might be reserved for different activities, some of which require more attention than others, and some of which permit more movement than others. As a result, students are able to engage in a variety of activities within one room, and the teacher does not have to enforce the strictest standards uniformly throughout the room.

Another way to control antecedents is to analyze sequences or chains of behavior. A person who wants to smoke less may find that he or she regularly smokes while relaxing at the table at the end of a meal. By leaving the table immediately after finishing the food and moving to a setting where smoking seldom occurs, the smoker interrupts the behavioral chain at the step that precedes smoking. Note also that this technique implies no moralistic judgment of the behavior of the person ("I don't even have the willpower to quit smoking"). Instead, it analyzes and attempts to control events associated with the troublesome behavior.

One attempt to induce new behavior by modifying a behavioral chain involved a 4-year-old girl. Although she was fully toilet trained she seemed never to remember to flush the toilet when she should, a matter of some irritation to others in her family. She was repeatedly scolded and ordered back to flush, but next time the toilet remained unflushed again. Finally, a behaviorally sophisticated uncle required her to repeat the entire chain of behavior: ". . . she was to make believe to the extent that she was to take down her pants, climb up on the toilet, imagine she was just finishing, get off the toilet, pull up her pants, then flush the toilet and rejoin the adults. This exercise worked; the child gives every sign that she will grow up to be a happily married lady who flushes the toilet a lot" (Homme et al., 1968, p. 429). The exercise successfully increased the frequency of a particular behavior by strengthening the relationship between that behavior and its antecedent. Scolding and moralistic judgments were avoided.

This procedure may be helpful to teachers wherever behavioral chains can be identified. Performing laboratory routines, solving math problems, preparing to go home at the end of the day—all these are situations in which occurrence of a desirable behavior may be made more likely by rehearsal of the behavioral chain in which it occurs.

The control of consequences.   A repeated finding from behavioral research is that behavior followed by positive consequences is likely to increase in frequency. Behavior followed by negative or neutral consequences, on the other hand, is likely to decrease. (Because negative or punishing consequences have certain undesirable side effects, they are to be avoided when possible.) A teacher who is in a position to make particular consequences contingent upon particular behaviors can exert a powerful influence on those behaviors.

One demonstration of these principles occurred in a nursery school. A 3-year-old girl spent most of her nursery school time crawling or crouching rather than walking. Classroom observation showed that the teachers' attention was often drawn by that problem behavior but was seldom drawn when the child stood or walked. Contingencies were arranged so that teachers ignored the child when she was crawling or crouching but gave her warm attention when she was standing, running, or walking. Within a week "off-feet" behavior declined from 80% to a proportion similar to that of her peers. As an experimental control, attention was then made contingent on crawling or crouching, as before, and withheld for standing and walking; soon she was again off her feet 80% of the time. A final reversal of rewards put her back on her feet 62% of the time by the fourth day. Her relations with others in the group improved, too, once she was not spending most of her time crawling (Harris, Johnston, Kelley, & Wolf, 1964).

A much more ambitious application of the control of consequences involved an institution for delinquents. Environmental contingencies of reinforcement were redesigned for residents of the National Training School for Boys in Washington, D. C. The major change was the virtual elimination of aversive control: nobody was *required* to do anything. "A boy might, if he wished, 'go on relief'; he could eat nutritious if uninteresting food, sleep on a pad in a dormitory, and spend each day sitting on a bench. He could greatly improve his way of life, however, by earning points exchangeable for more interesting food, a private room, a television set, admission to the game room, a trip away from the institution, and so on. Points could be earned by working in the kitchen or by performing janitorial services, *but most readily by studying and learning.* Right answers were worth points" (Skinner, 1969a, p. 21). Two important results were observed. The first was improved morale. Behavior improved, and in addition a great deal of useful work got done despite the absence of aversive controls. The second result enhanced the effectiveness of the institution. Boys who had believed they were dull experienced success in acquiring important skills, many of them learning a great deal quite rapidly. Their new skills improved their chances of good adjustment upon release.

It is important to realize that antecedents and consequences do not *cause* behavior in the same way that an electric shock causes a reflex response. We have been discussing the results of *learning*: associations between a particular behavior and certain antecedents and between that behavior and certain consequences. Because these associations have been learned, often haphazardly, they can also be unlearned and otherwise modified. The experimental analysis of behavior seeks to document behavioral relationships and to determine effective ways of altering them. Behaviorists see particular behaviors as the results of a learning process rather than (moralistically) as expressions of the unbroken will of students.

TWIN OAKS: A COMMUNITY BASED ON BEHAVIORAL PSYCHOLOGY

In 1948, Skinner published *Walden Two*, a novel in which he described a residential community, nearly self-sufficient, based on the principles just described. The novel stimulated a number of experiments, and one resulted in Twin Oaks, a community in rural Virginia. It was established in 1967 and customarily has had 30 to 40 residents. A friend of mine returned from a visit to Twin Oaks with high enthusiasm. "It is the people," he said. "The people are lovable. They are gentle and concerned. Some more than others. But there is an atmosphere of quiet commitment, a sense of getting something together that no one else has got together yet." He felt that the excitement of Twin Oaks came from its explicit ideological commitment. "Not everyone would claim such beliefs for himself, but the core thrust is belief that answers to social questions come only from social experimentation and scientific observation of results of these experiments." Several features of life at Twin Oaks illustrate applications of behavioral principles.

First, consider how behavioral analysis assists with the practical matter of getting community work done. With the exception of a few who work outside the community, most members work a six-hour day at Twin Oaks. But each member decides what tasks to perform and when to put in that time. Depending on the nature of the task, some may put in more time than others. Payment is made in "labor credits." Each chore counts for a specified number of credits, and each member has a weekly quota of credits to earn. Members turn in requests for their preferred jobs. "The choice was great. For 2 credits, I could put away the groceries; for 1, draw up a menu, do auto repair or tractor maintenance. Under the large category of laundry, I could choose any one of four separate jobs: manning the automatic washer, ironing, overseeing the drying, or mending. Under the section 'Animals and Farm,' I could spray the cows; I could feed them hay; I could mind or milk them" (Houriet, 1971, pp. 293–294). Other jobs include making hammocks (hammocks are a major source of income for the community), making grocery-buying trips to town, printing, greeting visitors, and many more.

When requests for a particular job are too numerous, several steps can be taken. The immediate problem of who does the job that week is solved impartially, perhaps by the flip of a coin. The larger problem of supply and demand is solved by reducing the attractiveness of that job by assigning fewer credits to it the next week. Jobs in which no one shows interest are given additional credits.

Although details of the labor-credit system change from time to time, the basic principle described by Skinner in *Walden Two* is preserved: pay is greatest for the least desirable work. Equality of work is based not on one dimension such as time-on-job but on a weighted combination of (1) time, (2) the objective characteristics of the job, and (3) the subjective evaluation of its appeal.

Reinforcement for the worker comes from the satisfaction of completing a job, from the accumulation of labor credits, and in accountability for the quality of work. In order to facilitate social reinforcement, signs are sometimes posted, such as "This room is cleaned this week by _____."

Elimination of undesirable behavior calls for strategies different from those that reinforce desirable behavior. When the community unanimously identified smoking as undesirable (because of both health and cost), they altered their physical environment to make smoking less attractive. The tobacco tin and roller—allowances are not sufficient to permit members to buy commercial cigarettes—were put in a little-used location, one which was uncomfortably hot during the day. Consensus kept them there. Note that the first strategy is to reduce consumption (alter behavior). Once people smoke less, it is assumed that attitudes about their habit and about themselves will change. Change in the physical environment is assumed to precede psychological change.

Problems of interpersonal relations are also dealt with by behavioral analysis. For example, there is a mechanism for handling complaints. When a member shirks job assignments or does them poorly or otherwise creates tension, a mediator is available. The mediator is called the "Generalized Bastard."

> His job is to be officially nasty. For example, suppose that a certain member has a habit of letting his work partner do the dirty part of the work and of skipping out on the last ten minutes of cleanup on a shared job. If this happens once or twice, his partner begins to resent it. He hates to say, "Hey, how about doing a full share of this job for a change?" In order to avoid a building up of resentment, the complaining member goes to the Generalized Bastard. His job is to carry the complaint to the offender, which he can do in an objective way [quoted in Roberts, 1971, pp. 94–95].

The norm of communication is to be as direct and open as possible. Gossip is prohibited. The Code to which all members subscribe states "We will not discuss the personal affairs of other members or speak negatively of other members when they are not present or in the presence of a third party."

Twin Oaks has been concerned with its own development and survival, with creating its version of the good life. But its mind-set and its applications of the technology of behavior deserve consideration for use in other settings. Is life at Twin Oaks merely a curiosity? What implications does it have for nursery school classes, for college dorms, for family life?

SOME CLAIMS FOR THE BEHAVIORAL APPROACH

In essence, the behavioral approach in education calls for the teacher to identify desirable student behaviors and to control the antecedents or consequences of those behaviors. The teacher is to avoid aversive control (scolding, punishment, and the threat of punishment) as much as possible. The teacher looks toward the environment (antecedents and consequences) for the causes of behavior rather than toward some quality within the student such as motivation or cooperation.

Later in this chapter we will review some objections to this point of view. But first, I want to summarize five of the claims made on behalf of the behavioral approach. (The first four categories are based on Nolan, 1974).

Equitable rewards.   The behavioral approach extends rewards to those who otherwise seldom receive them. Who is usually most rewarded in school? Troublemakers receive attention, which, ironically, reinforces their undesirable behavior. Those from advantaged homes who have already learned from family example how to be good students receive praise and high grades. On the other hand, a disadvantaged child, lacking incentives from home, may feel that the hard work necessary in learning to read is not worthwhile. That child may be left out of the reward system unless material rewards (candy, free time, a toy) are used to initiate study behaviors. Later on, grades, if they come often enough, may be sufficient to maintain study behavior. Eventually, personal satisfaction—what the advantaged child has had all along—may become sufficient.

Basic to a behavioral program is reinforcement for *every* child, even the slowest, who engages in study and who demonstrates some learning. Children respond in different ways to different reinforcers, and care must be taken to choose, or have the child choose, rewards that are powerful. With appropriate rewards for every child, social-class differences in rate of learning can be greatly narrowed.

Avoidance of punishment.   A second characteristic of the behavioral approach is the reduction or even elimination of punishment from the educational process. Since the likelihood of learning is reduced when there is constant disruption, it is natural to punish disruptive behavior in order to create a learning atmosphere. But punishment is only temporarily effective; over time it may actually raise the total amount of disruption.

Making positive consequences contingent upon *productive* student behavior reduces disruption in two ways. First, teachers do not scold those who are disruptive. As a result, disruptive behavior is not rewarded with attention, and so it decreases. (To use the behavioral term, it is *extinguished.*) Second, productive learning behavior is incompatible with disruption, so disruption automatically decreases as reinforcement produces increased attention, studying, and participation.

Consistency. Many of the principles of behavioral psychology seem like conventional wisdom. The notion of rewarding desirable student behavior has been endorsed and practiced by many teachers over many years. What is new in the behavioral approach is its systematic emphasis, beginning with careful observation of behavior and continuing with an intervention plan ensuring that reinforcers are appropriate, immediate, and consistent. Many well-disposed teachers reward desirable behavior, to be sure, but do so too infrequently, or after too much delay, or with a reinforcer that is inappropriate for the particular child.

The importance of carefully observing and recording behavior can hardly be overstated. Some teachers, for example, were perplexed by their first graders' standing up too much. They were perplexed because the children did sit down when asked, and yet more and more children seemed to be standing. An observational record demonstrated just that: the more often the teacher said "Sit down" (and the children did sit down), the more often the children stood up. With the observational record available it was possible to understand what was happening. "Sit down" served to control an antecedent and to cue sitting. But "Sit down" also carried the teacher's attention, which reinforced pupils for the preceding response, standing up. Attention is a powerful reinforcer, and so standing increased. Since the children did sit down, the teachers thought that this command (really an example of attempted aversive control) was working, but in fact the situation grew worse in the long run (cited in Becker, 1973).

Suppose Jimmy is irritating the teacher by being out of his seat during a spelling lesson. He bothers other students, too, and has been failing tests. First the teacher must determine what precedes out-of-seat behavior (antecedents). Then an appropriate positive consequence must be identified. Perhaps Jimmy likes to carry messages to the office. An appropriate reinforcer would be the privilege of delivering the class attendance report to the office when he scores 80% or higher on a test. To earn that score requires study, and study is incompatible with wandering around the classroom. Thus Jimmy should be less disruptive and should also learn more.

Note how inappropriate it would be to deal with this situation in the common aversive way. Ordinarily the teacher might scold Jimmy, shaming him back to his seat. Finally the teacher might lose patience and send Jimmy with a note to the principal's office. But since Jimmy *likes* to deliver notes (the principal isn't there half the time, and when he is his lectures aren't so bad), the intended punishment actually reinforces his disruptive behavior. It is hardly appropriate and consistent reinforcement (Nolan, 1974).

Only careful behavioral analysis and consistent use of reinforcers are likely to produce the desired results with Jimmy.

Individual attention. Another traditional virtue of education, attention to the needs of individual learners, is enhanced by the behavioral approach. In order to determine what level of behavior to reward and what reinforcer to use, the teacher must have considerable information about a learner. Jimmy's teacher, for example, needed to know what learning capacity he had in order to choose the 80% score level and what privileges he valued in order to choose the messenger reinforcer. This strategy would obviously not have been appropriate for a child willing to learn but mentally incapable of the tasks or for a shy child who seldom wanders far from the classroom. The procedure is fine for Jimmy, who has the capacity and the study skills but not the attention span.

The behavioral approach requires knowledge of and respect for the characteristics of each individual in order to identify appropriate tasks and appropriate rewards for progress on those tasks.

Research support. The behavioral approach originated in the laboratory with research on animals. Standards of rigor and control characteristic of laboratory research also characterize these applied behavioral studies of humans in natural settings. Hundreds of studies have been done, and they provide persuasive evidence that the behavioral approach is effective. Indeed, there may be more research support for educational applications of behavioral psychology than for any other educational procedure.

This research is done sometimes with individuals and sometimes with groups. The latter include classes, families, and work groups. Classroom research has involved classes of normal children, with a variety of ethnic and social-class characteristics, from preschool through college, as well as classes of children with learning disabilities or personality disorders. Research designs may control antecedents or reinforcers; they may use material reinforcers (candy, money), activity reinforcers (free time, specified privileges), or social reinforcers (smiles, attention). Elaborate "token economies" may be set up, in which appropriate behavior is rewarded by tokens. Tokens are accumulated and subsequently exchanged for other reinforcers. Reports of behavioral research in educational settings appear in such periodicals as the *Journal of Applied Behavior Analysis* and in such volumes as *Behavior Modification in Education* (Thoresen, 1973). The latter includes chapters on most of the topics mentioned above.

Behavioral research typically involves four stages. The first is a *baseline* period for collecting information about the frequency of the behavior in question and about the events that precede and follow that behavior. Baseline information often helps to specify the target behavior more precisely and to determine what changes in contingencies are indicated. The second stage is the *intervention* period, during which the new contingencies are introduced. Intervention may affect antecedents or consequences. It may involve a precise schedule of reinforcers and perhaps a token economy. Great care is taken to be precise and consistent: reinforcement should occur when and only when the desired behavior occurs. The third research stage, *reversal*, involves changing the contingencies back to the preintervention stage. Recall that for the nursery school child this meant once again providing teacher attention for off-feet behavior, with the result that the desired on-feet behavior decreased as off-feet behavior increased. Reversals may seem a heartless way to deal with research participants, but they are an important component of research, because they demonstrate that what produced changes in behavior was the intervention rather than some factor such as the passage of time. (In research with groups, reversals may be avoided through the use of a control group.) Reversals should be brief, in any case, and quickly followed by the fourth stage, *intervention reintroduced*. For the girl in nursery school, reinstating reinforcement for on-feet behavior caused that behavior to increase again, thus confirming that results were due solely to the behavioral intervention.

An illustration of these four stages is provided by a large-scale study involving all students and teachers in an elementary school in Atlanta, a school with substandard achievement, a high delinquency rate, and a high proportion of poverty families. The 14 teachers received training in the behavioral principles enumerated earlier in this chapter, particularly (1) ignoring disruptive behavior (unless it is severe), (2) reinforcing desired behaviors and those incompatible with the behaviors to be eliminated, and (3) being certain that reinforcement (including verbal praise) is immediate. The study compared these 14 teachers (experimental) with 8 untrained teachers (control) in a nearby school. Observers visited the classroom of each teacher both before and after training and recorded incidences of positive teacher behaviors, negative teacher behaviors, student disruption, and student attention.

Before training (baseline), the students of both experimental and control teachers experienced many times more negative events (sarcasm, criticism, withdrawal of privileges, and so on). The intervention reduced the number of negative events and increased the number of positive events in the experimental classes so that they became more nearly equal: 11 of the 14 teachers reduced negative events by 50% or more. Control teachers, on the other hand, changed little. What of student behavior? The intervention reduced student disruption in experimental classes; no change occurred in control classes. Student attention to their tasks increased in every experimental class. The average increase for experimental classes was 17%, but it was only 3% in control classes.

I believe this study is especially important because it included all teachers in a school rather than just those who volunteered. Training increased time on task for students of every teacher and had additional strong benefits for 11 of the 14 teachers. Thus the study demonstrates not only that the behavioral approach makes significant changes but that it can do so for the great majority of teachers who have been trained (Thompson, Brassell, Persons, Tucker, & Rollins, 1974).

Widespread acceptance of the behavioral approach does not necessarily come because research has demonstrated its effectiveness or because of other advantages claimed. It is possible to object to the behavioral approach on practical grounds—for example, that the approach is too expensive or otherwise not feasible. It is also possible to object on philosophical grounds—for example, because the behavioral approach gives too much power to teachers. These and other objections are discussed in the next section.

OBJECTIONS TO THE BEHAVIORAL APPROACH

Discussions about behavioral psychology are often quite heated. In fact, the term used by many behaviorists, *behavior modification*, is sometimes employed by other psychologists as an insult. I have avoided that term so far in this chapter partly because of the negative connotations it has acquired, but primarily because of its lack of specificity. Behavior modification includes applied behavioral psychology, to be sure, but it may also refer to changing behavior by surgery, medication, imprisonment, legislation, and other means. Our discussion is concerned only with the modification of behavior by the control of antecedents or consequences— that is, modification of behavior using principles of behavioral psychology.

The behaviorist position apparently touches on deeply held values and thereby stimulates discussions that are sometimes very emotional. Behaviorist writers, particularly Skinner, characteristically write with a bluntness of style that may seem to oversimplify very complex matters. In the following passage, Skinner contrasts the traditional view of behavior with what he calls the scientific view.

> In the traditional picture a person perceives the world around him, selects features to be perceived, discriminates among them, judges them good or bad, changes them to make them better (or, if he is careless, worse), and may be held responsible for his action and justly rewarded or punished for its consequences. In the scientific picture a person is a member of a species shaped by evolutionary contingencies of survival, displaying behavioral processes which bring him under the control of the environment in which he lives, and largely under the control of a social environment which he and millions of others like him have constructed and maintained during the evolution of a culture. The direction of the controlling relation is reversed: a person does not act upon the world, the world acts upon him [Skinner, 1971, p. 211].

In that passage Skinner equates the behavioral position with "the scientific picture" and contrasts it with the traditional views that most of his readers hold. His assertion that the controlling relationship is the world acting upon the person rather than the person acting upon the world is quite remarkable. If the relationship is as he suggests, many of our beliefs about human autonomy, freedom, and individual dignity must be reconsidered. That is precisely his point, and is proclaimed by the very title of his best-selling book *Beyond Freedom and Dignity*.

It is entirely appropriate that behavioral views be subject to extensive debate. I shall summarize three categories of objections, one primarily philosophical, one primarily practical, and one primarily empirical.

THE PHILOSOPHICAL OBJECTIONS

The behavioral approach carries with it certain assumptions about the nature of organisms, including human beings, and about the relationships of humans with one another and with their environments.

Philosophical objections to the adequacy of the behavioral view revolve around the notion of "control" in human relationships. Skinner seems to imply that the relationship between an experimenter and a subject is an adequate model of human relationships. That relationship is very circumscribed. The subject is dependent and submissive, holds a very short time perspective, and performs only assigned tasks (Argyris, 1971). Can this model be appropriately applied to the relationship between teacher and student?

Critics contend that this is not an adequate view of human relationships. Much of the time persons should confront their environment rather than submit to it, they say; to be effective, the behavioral position must reinforce dependence and submission. ". . . Skinner's many examples assume that the world is populated with people who have power and with those who do not, and that is the way things should and must remain" (Argyris, 1971, p. 563).

Behaviorists' slogans and publications often lend credence to this view. One three-volume compilation of research is called *The Control of Human Behavior* (Ulrich, Stachnik, & Mabry, 1974). A manual for parents carries the title *How to Make Johnny Want to Obey* (Beltz, 1971).

In response, some behaviorists assert that their position is a technology, rather than a philosophy. One collection of Skinner's writing is entitled *The Technology of Teaching*, implying a set of procedures for alleviating problems and increasing effectiveness. Since all teachers are in the business of modifying behavior, whether or not they call it by that name, the behavioral approach should be judged according to its effectiveness in a given situation relative to that of other procedures with the same purpose. Behavioral principles can be misused, as can any other technology, but they are not inherently inadequate or dangerous.

Another response to the philosophical objections is that the behaviorist is not attempting to control behavior directly, as is a teacher who threatens "If you don't start studying, I'll . . . ." Instead, the behaviorist controls antecedents and consequences of behavior; the learner is never compelled to respond to those contingencies. That distinction is a very subtle one, however, and most critics feel it does not deal fairly with their objections.

THE PRACTICAL OBJECTIONS

Those who object on practical grounds offer arguments that behavioral procedures are limited in their impact, too expensive to institute, or otherwise not feasible. A major theme in these objections is that behavioral procedures are too narrow in their outcomes. Behavioral approaches are said to set up an artificial situation in which only specific low-level learning can be attained. They require behaviors or subject matter to be analyzed into very small steps, as if everyone learned in the same way, although at different rates. It is not practical, say the critics, to organize all schooling in this way. Normal children need freedom to develop imagination and creativity. Programs based on behavioral principles cannot produce well-rounded learners.

In response, behaviorists defend the virtues of specificity.

> To say that a program is to "impart knowledge," "train rational powers," or "make students creative" is not to identify the changes which are actually to be brought about . . . . We do not impart knowledge; we generate behavior said to show the possession of knowledge. We do not improve abilities or strengthen rational powers; we make it more likely that the student will show the behavior from which abilities and powers are inferred. When goals are properly specified, the teacher knows what he is to do and, later, whether he has done it. Behavioral objectives remove much of the mystery from education, and teachers may feel demeaned when their task is reduced to less awesome dimensions. But their loss is more than offset by a greater sense of achievement [Skinner, 1969b, p. 95].

Without question, behaviorally oriented education provides greater clarity about expectation and rewards than does traditional education. Behaviorists believe this explicitness to be a virtue because it lets learners know precisely where they stand. They contrast it with some free or open schools where teachers arrange the environment so that children will do what the teachers wish, but where the teachers' influence is kept so subtle that children are likely to feel they have made their own free choice. Children cannot defend themselves against teachers' influence if they do not know what that influence is (Bereiter, 1973). In this case, the behavioral approach is said to be not only more practical but, because it is more explicit, also more ethical.

THE EMPIRICAL OBJECTIONS

A final category of objections to the behavioral approach raises issues based on results of empirical research. In this section we will review research that suggests some limits of the behavioral approach. The research is classified according to the three settings in which it was done: settings where participation was coerced, settings where participation was not coerced but was not truly voluntary, and settings where participation was truly voluntary. (These categories are based on Russell, 1974.)

Coercive settings. An extreme example of a coercive setting is a prisoner-of-war camp. The prisoner *must* submit to any modification of behavior imposed by the authorities. Much of the purported success of behavioral procedures comes from settings such as prisons, hospitals, and schools. If a token economy is set up in one of these institutions, persons usually participate without protest under the subtle pressures of the situation. A student may have the legal right to refuse participation in such a school program, but that right is very seldom exercised.

Two important conclusions emerge from reviews of this research. First, effects seldom generalize beyond the experimental environment (Levine & Fasnacht, 1974; Russell, 1974; Wildman & Wildman, 1975). That is, systematic application of behavioral principles may help teachers to increase the proportion of time students spend on task, and as a result students may earn higher grades; but students' time on task will decrease once they leave that teacher and that class. Even though they acquired some subject-matter knowledge, they may not have learned study skills that generalize to other situations. Nor have they learned the intrinsic rewards of learning. Probably what they have learned were the rules for success *in that situation*. In other words, the desired behavior patterns and study skills will be performed only when particular contingencies are in effect. This does not mean that behavioral procedures do not work, but it implies a need for caution about expecting reinforced behaviors to generalize to other settings.

Second, extrinsic reinforcement may actually reduce intrinsic motivation (Levine & Fasnacht, 1974). That is, learners with initially high motivation to work on school tasks may, as a result of a token economy, come to depend instead on external reinforcement. They learn to complete tasks to obtain a reward rather than because they like the tasks. These findings do not deny that the behavioral approach works with students of low motivation who would otherwise not engage in the task; they merely warn against a needless and possibly harmful misdirected use of behavioral procedures with students who are already motivated.

In summary, research on behavioral procedures in coercive institutional settings has identified two cautions about their effectiveness, namely that they should be avoided with students who are already motivated and that changes in performance should not be expected to generalize beyond the situations in which reinforcement contingencies are in effect. These limits imply that fears of behavioral psychology as a brainwashing tool are unfounded, since brainwashing must be coercive and must endure beyond the training situation.

Noncoercive settings.   In other behavioral research, the participant is initially a volunteer but does not choose the particular strategies to be used. Instead, the experimenter creates an experimental situation in

which the subject participates. For example, the subject may be asked to construct and speak a series of sentences, and the experimenter will reinforce, perhaps by a nod of the head, a specific bit of verbal behavior. Subjects are not informed of the contingency; nevertheless, they show an increase in the frequency of the reinforced verbal behavior. Those findings are remarkable because they appear to demonstrate that everyday behavior can be modified in unconscious, perhaps sinister ways, without the subject's knowledge. In fact, however, such conditioning does not occur without awareness. Instead, the subject actively forms hypotheses about what the experimenter wants; conditioning occurs only if the subject is able to figure out what the experimenter wants and then decides to act in that way (Russell, 1974).

These findings are reassuring because they suggest that behavioral programs aimed at modifying everyday behaviors work only if learners are willing to let them work. Ultimate control belongs to the learner, not to the behavior modifier.

Voluntary settings. The final type of setting is one in which a person is motivated to change in a particular way and seeks professional help to do so. Research on psychotherapy conducted according to behavioral principles is an example of this type of setting. Both patients and therapists report positive changes. Behavioral therapy does produce greater change, at least where specific behavioral symptoms have been targeted, than do other therapeutic approaches. But it is difficult to know how much of the effect is due to behavioral principles as such and how much is due to nonspecific factors such as suggestion or the attention of the therapist.

A therapist's office is quite different from a classroom, of course. It may be difficult to imagine a student coming to a behaviorally oriented teacher and saying "I haven't been studying hard enough lately. Please modify my behavior." And yet behavioral principles may be useful in just that voluntary situation. We shall consider some research on behavioral *self*-modification in the next section of this chapter.

This review of research on the behavioral approach suggests that the approach has some severe limitations. As a sinister controlling mechanism, it poses little threat to whatever freedom individuals possess. Its effectiveness depends on the subject's cooperation and may not generalize beyond the coercive training setting. On the other hand, in a cooperative setting, behavioral principles may permit persons to enhance the control they have over themselves. None of these limitations deny that behavioral programs are useful for changing behavior within particular settings, as the study in Atlanta schools (Thompson et al., 1974) demonstrates. But their usefulness may be limited to the particular circumstances in which contingencies are in effect.

BEHAVIORAL SELF-MODIFICATION

All educational and therapy systems claim to be interested in promoting self-direction. Students are expected to learn not only about subject matter but also about themselves as learners. They are expected to become more capable of directing their own learning in the future. Therapists expect that the insights gained in therapy permit clients to handle stressful situations more effectively the next time such situations occur. Yet most education and therapy begin with a highly limiting definition of the relationship between learner and teacher or between client and therapist, a relationship that puts the latter very much in charge of the former. The learner submits to the authority and expertise of the teacher, a relationship that is likely to foster dependence rather than independence.

An alternative approach is to assist students to learn principles of self-management, which can be applied to problem situations. If these principles are effective in a wide range of situations, from study problems to dealing with anxiety, the learner has acquired tools to solve problems without the direct intervention of an expert. Because principles characterizing the behavioral approach are relatively concise and easily communicated, there has been considerable effort by behaviorists to design programs for enhancing self-control. These behavior-modification programs are aimed not at the modification of other people's behavior but at the modification of one's own behavior.

SELF-MODIFICATION PROJECTS
FOR COLLEGE STUDENTS

Behavioral self-modification projects are appropriately introduced into courses in which behavioral psychology is studied. Such an experience requires not only cognitive mastery of behavioral principles, but application of them as well. Students who are likely to be asked to use behavior modification in their subsequent careers find this experience especially helpful, because changing their own behavior helps reveal the ethical questions involved in behavior modification.

To illustrate the use of self-modification projects, I will describe courses in which we have used them as student assignments. Students are quizzed on the content of a text on behavioral psychology (Watson & Tharp, 1972). Then each student chooses a personal problem area to work on and tries to identify specific related behaviors that should be increased, decreased, or otherwise altered. During the baseline period, the student keeps a careful record of that target behavior, plotting the frequency of its occurrence on a graph. Next the student determines what frequency of the target behavior is an appropriate goal and designs an intervention in which antecedents and/or consequences are altered. Continuing behavioral observations show what effect the intervention has had. All this is done with a minimum of consultation with course instructors. Plans may be revised, depending on progress. Eventually the target behavior should become well established and the contingency plan can be gradually eliminated.

The project of one of our students illustrates each of these stages. An undergraduate woman was distressed by her habitual use of the word "bullshit" in casual conversation. Her baseline self-observations revealed that she used the word an average of 17 times a day, a distressingly high frequency in her opinion. She further specified an emotional condition that accompanied her utterance of "bullshit." At those times she felt embarrassed and conspicuous; often her hand trembled.

She set what she hoped was a realistic goal of five to seven uses of the word per day, although fewer would have been even more acceptable. She expected that meeting her behavioral goals would also alleviate her emotional distress. Intervention consisted of reinforcing (with sweets) successive reductions of the target behavior coupled with reinforcement for utterance of incompatible words—for example, "baloney." The target behavior declined steadily over a four-week period to an average of four utterances per day. These behavioral results were acceptable and were accompanied by positive emotional conditions. "The methods I employed were very effective," she told us. "I now use the target comment less than four times a day and my use of other words is increasing daily as I concentrate more and more on this new aspect of my vocal behavior . . . I now feel much better about myself when I talk to others" (McGaghie & Menges, 1975, p. 57). These changes were still present eight weeks later, according to a follow-up telephone interview.

What target behaviors and reinforcers do students choose? Figure 2–1 classifies the target behaviors of 167 of our students. Most frequently chosen were study habits, accounting for about one-fourth of all projects. Other personal habits were popular targets. They included behaviors involved in diet, smoking, exercise, and appearance. A few projects (8%) involved relationships with other people.

The reinforcers used in these projects are classified in Figure 2–2. (More than one reinforcer was used by 107 of the 167 students.) Recreational activities of several types, solitary or social, accounted for most reinforcers. Food and drink reinforcers were also popular. Purchases were a common reinforcer for those who employed token systems.

We have found a success rate of more than 70% for these projects. This estimate is based on students' own reports, since it is not practical to make independent observations of each student's behavior. Student esti-

Figure 2-1.   Target behaviors selected for self-modification

Target Behavior	No. of Projects	% of Total
Study habits (24,16)[a]	40	24%
Weight (6,17)	23	14%
Self-discipline	22	13%
music practice (2,6); saving money (1,3); procrastination (1,2); managing time (0,2); neatness (0,2); impatience (0,1); memorizing song lyrics (1,0); transcendental meditation (1,0)		
Smoking (11,10)	21	13%
Exercise (6,13)	19	11%
Cosmetic	14	8%
nail biting (0,7); posture (1,2); gum chewing (0,2); beard pulling (1,0); fingernail scratching (0,1)		
Dietary improvement (4,9)	13	8%
Human relations	13	8%
family (2,1); lover (0,3); self-criticism (1,2); spouse (1,2); peers (0,1)		
Repetitive speech (0,2)	2	1%
Totals	167	100%

Note: N = 167 (63 males and 104 females). Percentages are inexact because of rounding.
[a]The first number represents males; the second represents females.

mates should be honest, especially since course credit for a project does not depend on the success of the project. A well-understood project failure may be as profitable a learning experience as a project success.

Students choose what appear to be relatively uncomplicated personal habits for their initial self-modification projects. That does not mean, however, that behavioral self-modification is inapplicable to interpersonal behaviors or to thoughts and feelings, which are not directly observable. Indeed the student whose project was described above reported considerable emotional satisfaction as a consequence of behavior change. Other researchers have worked with thoughts and emotions directly. For example, several students who reported feelings of depression, confirmed by personality-test scores, are described by Tharp, Watson, and Kaya (1974). One student decided that her depression was connected with an inability to express honestly her thoughts and feelings. She began systematically reinforcing "honest" statements, made either aloud or to herself. The frequency of these statements increased greatly, and a subsequent personality test indicated no depression.

Self-modification projects seem to be useful for teaching the principles of behavioral psychology through application of those principles. But

Figure 2-2. Reinforcers used for self-modification

Reinforcer	No. of Projects
Individual recreation	108
television viewing (20,18)[a]; listening to music (13,13); free time (3,9); pleasure reading (7,4); guitar playing (3,4); walks (4,3); sewing (0,4); daydreaming (0,1); piano playing (0,1); playing pinball machines (1,0)	
Social reinforcement	76
visits with friends (7,24); praise and attention from family and friends (11,18); use of telephone (4,9); sexual responsiveness from partner (1,1); weekend trips to family (0,1)	
Food	53
candy and snack foods (9,13); meals (13,9); dining out (0,4); chewing gum (0,2); fruit (1,0); ice cream (0,1); strawberry yogurt (1,0)	
Interpersonal recreation	39
sports participation (14,2); weekend dates (3,4); film (movie) viewing (3,4); concerts (2,1); playing pool (3,0); vists to nightclubs (2,1)	
Purchases	31
clothing (1,12); books (3,6); records (2,4); flowers (1,1); extravagant items (0,1)	
Drink	20
alcoholic beverages (7,3); soft drinks (3,3); coffee (0,2); water (2,0)	
Miscellaneous	34
sleep (4,4); showers (0,7); opening the mail (2,3); writing letters (1,3); money (0,2); appearance of nails (0,1); Bible reading (0,1); charitable contributions (0,1); early termination of evening study (1,0); marijuana (0,1); nightly pleasurable activities (1,0); prayer (1,0); washing hair (0,1)	

Note: 107 participants used multiple reinforcers; 94 participants used point or token systems.
[a]The first number represents males; the second represents females.

research is needed to learn more about the effective components of the procedures, and some research issues are described in the next section.

SOME PROBLEMS FOR RESEARCH

The use of behavioral principles to alter feelings, thoughts, and other nonobservable phenomena is one area deserving further research (see Meichenbaum & Cameron, 1974). Other issues also deserve attention if the process of self-modification is to be better understood.

Problems of selection and prediction.   Not all people are equally successful with projects, yet little is known about how successful self-modifiers differ from those who are unsuccessful. Such variables as sex and academic aptitude are not strong predictors of success (McGaghie, Menges, & Dobroski, 1976). Perhaps future research will show that attitudes about behavioral psychology or personality variables are important. Once a profile of the successful self-modifier can be drawn, it would be possible to select those most likely to succeed. For others, alternative approaches to self-control (such as the mutual-aid groups discussed in a later chapter) might be employed.

Problems of observation. Developing an adequate self-modification plan requires accurate observation of one's own behavior. Some persons are less willing or able than others to be accurate; for them, training programs in self-observation may be needed. For example, an eight-hour multimedia workshop has been developed for training teachers to accurately observe and record their own behaviors while they teach (Hendricks, Thoresen, & Hubbard, 1974).

With some of our students, we have found that behavioral change may occur prior to intervention solely as a result of self-observation. Observing and recording baseline behaviors often reveals inappropriate antecedents or consequences that are not particularly difficult to change. Identifying them during the baseline period is sometimes sufficient to bring about change. Therefore, additional research is needed on the relative importance of the observation and intervention stages (see Kazdin, 1974).

Problems of persistence and generalization. A third area requiring research deals with (1) the persistence over time of change in the target behavior and (2) generalization of self-modification skills to new target behaviors.

Since our students are completing a project for course credit, they no doubt feel some pressure from the instructor and fellow students to devote effort to the project and to show positive results. We try to minimize such pressure by not "requiring" success and we find no correlation between reported success and student ratings of the course. We do, however, encourage students to do high-quality projects, and we encourage them to support one another. Once students leave behind that supportive situation, the behavioral change may also be left behind, although an eight-week follow-up with 49 students did show a high level of persistence (McGaghie, Menges, & Dobroski, 1976). More long-term studies are needed.

Generalizing to new situations and new target behaviors is another vexing problem. Many of our students say they plan to use self-modification skills in the future, and some have already identified target behaviors for those future efforts, but it is uncertain whether they can carry out these interventions without the help of the instructor or the support of other students. Medical practitioners are particularly concerned with self-management—for example, taking medication regularly, altering diet, and performing exercise. Since most of us are faced with such medical directives from time to time, training in generalizable skills of self-modification would be useful. More research is necessary with medical problems and with persons of diverse educational and social-class backgrounds to determine factors that enhance generalizability.

SELF-MODIFICATION AND OBJECTIONS
TO THE BEHAVIORAL APPROACH

Behavioral self-modification has been presented as a positive use of behavioral psychology. It is appropriate to examine behavioral self-modification in light of the objections to the behavioral approach that were discussed earlier.

The philosophical objection: The nature of control. The behavioral view implies that human relationships involve controllers and controllees and must do so if behavioral procedures are to be effective. Critics contend that this is an inadequate view of human nature and human relationships and fear that behavioral influence may be exerted against one's will, since only the controller determines the nature and direction of the influence. Many institutional applications of behavioral procedures depend on such authoritarian relationships, as research described in this chapter illustrates.

To the extent that the goals of controller and controllee are congruent, that objection loses its validity. Such congruence does not exist when the teacher alone defines "good" behavior and then controls antecedents and consequences in order to increase the probability of good behavior and reduce the probability of bad behavior. But consider another possibility. Suppose a student, distressed about frequently getting into trouble, identifies a behavior-change goal and with the teacher plans some reinforcement contingencies to reach that goal. This situation is considerably different, because the relationship is collaborative and the learner is exerting significant control. Or imagine a college student who avoids taking a suggested college course in which readings, tests, and papers are planned by the professor and are the same for all students. Instead the student designs an independent reading experience and completes a large amount of work using self-planned and self-administered reinforcement. The professor merely advises and approves the student's initiative.

In both these examples a relationship in which a teacher customarily attempts to control a learner's behavior has become one in which the goals of the teacher and the goal of the learner are congruent. I believe that both examples represent appropriate uses of behavioral psychology as a technology. In these cases, the technology is an ethical and an effective mechanism for implementing mutually desired changes.

The practical objection: Narrowness of outcomes. Critics also contend that since the behavioral approach is most useful for specific objectives, it misses many important educational goals and consequently is not practical. But we have seen that the targets of self-modification are quite diverse. Alleviating depression is hardly trivial. Altering study habits may mean quite a lot to a student. Even reducing use of the word "bullshit" is significant if it results in feelings of greater self-esteem.

Nevertheless, these target behaviors are self-defined, and it is uncertain how adequately learners can plan desired learning experiences without strong direction from others. Many of the critics of behavioral procedures appear to be quite certain about how to increase creativity and critical thinking and other general (and valuable) characteristics in others. Yet those critics may be as authoritarian and controlling regarding their elusive goals as behaviorists are regarding their explicit objectives. Perhaps there is room for both the general and the specific and for both self-determined and teacher-determined goals and procedures.

Self-modification fares well against other practical objections. Self-modification skills can be taught to children as well as to adults. Because they are self-initiated and self-managed, self-modification skills require no special facilities or continuing staff. Their effectiveness is easily demonstrated. In short, they seem eminently practical.

The empirical objections: Generalization and motivation. As noted earlier, research on behavioral procedures has established two important limits to their effectiveness. First, although effects are strong while contingencies operate, effects usually do not generalize to other situations. For self-modification, however, the probability of generalization should be greater, because the learner is also the teacher. Since learners are fully informed about the contingencies and highly motivated toward change, successful self-modifiers may well be successful generalizers.

Second, research on token-economy systems suggests that a decrement in performance occurs for students who are already intrinsically motivated to perform desired behaviors. This finding, however, is irrelevant to self-modification, since a person already performing a task is unlikely to choose that behavior as a target for extrinsic reinforcement.

Recall that the success of studies in noncoercive settings, particularly studies that attempt to modify verbal behavior, depends on the subjects' being able to identify the desired behavior and on their intending to cooperate with the experimenter. That finding is a hopeful one for self-modification, since in a self-modification project the "subject" and the "experimenter" share the same intentions and knowledge. Whatever power the behavioral approach has is likely to be maximized under those conditions.

In my view the use of the behavioral approach for self-modification adequately withstands those criticisms of conventional behavior-modification programs that seem quite devastating. In self-modification the dignity and autonomy of the learner are preserved. Results can involve significant changes in significant behavior. And effects are maximized because the learner is fully aware of the contingencies. There are some questions about persistence and generalization of self-modification effects, but they are no more serious than questions raised about other behavioral procedures. Perhaps the most important advantage of the self-modification approach is that it enables persons who teach the principles of self-modification to pass the power of that technology on to others.

PSYCHOPOWER AND THE TEACHER AS CONTROLLER

"Power to the People" is a popular rallying cry for groups seeking increased political and economic power. Another kind of power, "psychopower," is suggested by the discussion in this chapter. Psychopower results from the successful application of psychological principles, in this case the technology of behavioral psychology. So far this power has been retained by those who devised the technology. I have argued in this chapter for instruction in self-modification so that "Power to the Psychologist" becomes "Power—psychopower—to the People."

Since teachers are among the people to whom this slogan refers, they should be trained in behavioral principles. Some teachers will direct psychopower *at* students as part of the teacher's controlling role. They may find good reason to reinforce submissive and conforming student behaviors. Their classrooms may be intolerably disruptive otherwise, and we have seen that carefully planned contingencies can make dramatic differences with poorly motivated students in compulsory education. Students may be as disruptive as usual away from those contingencies, but at least the classroom atmosphere will be one where subject-matter learning may occur.

Other teachers will share psychopower *with* students, by teaching self-modification skills to students and by reinforcing self-determined behavior. Results may be dramatic, since even disruptive children in first and second grades can be accurate in observing their own behavior. In one study, even when they knew that their self-observations were not being checked against those of a researcher, young children's observations were accurate and honest and disruptions were considerably reduced (Bolstad & Johnson, 1972).

Of course it is possible that psychopower will stimulate new power plays. Students may attempt to modify the behavior of each other, of teachers, or of family members. Gray, Graubard, and Rosenberg (1974) provide interesting examples of how easily this can happen. Unfortunately, such use of behavioral psychology would continue to exploit control relationships and to hoard rather than to share the power.

Another problem is that some people will be slower to master these skills than others. And these may well be the people who are most disadvantaged and powerless. In a discussion of sharing principles of persuasion with those who are the targets of persuasion, Argyris observes "In practice [this] argument is weak because the power people are much more likely to learn these principles than the poor people . . ." (Argyris, 1975, p. 479). Consequently, power relationships may not change significantly.

In this chapter I have described the teacher as controller. The focus of effort for teachers acting as controller is on observable behaviors of learners. The behaviors may be personal or social, desirable or undesirable, simple or complex. Teachers' efforts to control behavior conventionally call upon moral persuasion or the authority of the teachers' position. Behavioral psychology, by contrast, does not attempt to control behavior directly but attempts to alter it by changing its antecedents or consequences. The behavioral approach has been shown to lead to more productive classrooms and to higher levels of learning. Therefore the approach is useful for dealing with the important problem of student discipline.

When students master the skills of the behavioral approach, they may achieve a greater measure of self-control. Teachers may thus be controllers indirectly, by helping students reach behavioral goals that the students set for themselves.

FOR FURTHER READING

The undesirable conditions of much contemporary schooling are forcefully described in *How Children Fail* (Holt, 1964) and *Death at an Early Age* (Kozol, 1968). These books discuss private and urban public schools respectively.

Three texts that describe educational applications of behavioral principles in detail are *Teaching* (Becker, Englemann, & Thomas, 1975), *Instructional Applications of Behavioral Principles* (Gentile, Frazier, & Morris, 1975), and *Teaching/Discipline* (Madsen & Madsen, 1974). A more general overview is given in *Behavior Modification in Education* (Thoresen, 1973).

In addition to the fictional *Walden Two* (1948), Skinner's works include two nontechnical elaborations of his views, *Beyond Freedom and Dignity* (1971) and *About Behaviorism* (1974). His views on education are given in *The Technology of Teaching* (1968).

An account of life at Twin Oaks has been written by a participant, *A Walden Two Experiment: The First Five Years of Twin Oaks Community* (Kinkade, 1973).

Criticisms of the behavioral approach are presented in two books that contrast behavioral and humanistic views, *Humanism and/or Behaviorism in Education* (Kolesnik, 1975) and *Without/Within: Behaviorism and Humanism* (Matson, 1973).

Self-Directed Behavior (Watson & Tharp, 1972) is an exceptionally readable text and manual for self-modification projects. (See also Homme & Tosti, 1971; Williams & Long, 1975.) A somewhat more theoretical discussion of self-modification, together with reprints of research studies, is given in *Self-control: Power to the Person* (Mahoney & Thoresen, 1974). Thoresen and Coates (1976) discuss research with particular reference to self-control in therapy.

CHAPTER
THREE
THE TEACHER
AS MANAGER

Many teachers are somewhat uncomfortable in the role of controller described in the preceding chapter. They feel that students should *want* to learn, and they prefer to work with students who are already self-disciplined. They feel that teachers should be resources, advisers, and consultants. The role of manager accommodates these desires by emphasizing the larger learning environment and the teacher's role in structuring that environment.

As manager, the teacher is constantly making instructional decisions. Consider some of the decisions routinely made by teachers. Even before interacting with students, the teacher may use standardized test results and decide whether to work with a large group or with smaller groups within the class. Decisions must also be made about learning goals. Should the goals be primarily concerned with knowledge and information? Should they emphasize higher cognitive processes, such as problem solving? Should they deal with attitudes and values? With interpersonal behaviors? With motor skills? These planning decisions made in advance of instruction Mosston (1972) has referred to as "preimpact" decisions.

During the process of learning, the teacher must have materials and tasks available that are appropriate for the chosen goals. Decisions must be made about the rate of learning, which students to spend time with, where to be and where to position learners, and which behaviors to reinforce and which to ignore. Decisions related to this period, when learners are actively engaged in learning, Mosston calls "impact" decisions.

Finally, during the "postimpact" phase, there are decisions about the adequacy of learning. What information should be given as feedback by the teacher and by other students? What grading practices are appropriate? In addition to evaluating learning, the teacher looks at students' performance as a sign of the adequacy of instruction and may revise procedures based on that performance.

THREE KEY MANAGEMENT DECISIONS

All these managerial issues can be summarized in three key questions. First, what are the learning *objectives*—that is, what is to be learned (Mosston's preimpact decision)? Second, what are appropriate learning *activities* (impact decision)? Third, what is the desired *level* of learning; that is, how do we know when satisfactory learning has occurred (postimpact decision)?

Customarily each of these questions is answered by the teacher, who then instructs learners accordingly. Indeed, the role of teacher is often defined by the authority to decide these three aspects of learning: what, how, and how much. Some teachers are willing to share that decision-making role with learners, and decisions on learning objectives, activities, and evaluation are then made by both teacher and learners. Sometimes decisions are made primarily by learners alone. Increasing the decision responsibility of learners means that they have real (rather than artificial) choices to make and requires that they subsequently experience the consequences of those choices.

In this chapter, I describe six teaching/learning strategies in terms of the decision roles of teacher and learner. For each, I will ask who determines learning objectives, who chooses learning activities, and who decides when learning is satisfactory. The strategies range from one in which virtually all decisions are reserved by the teacher to one in which nearly all authority is held by the learner. In the first the teacher's decisions are preeminent. A chart at the end of the chapter (Figure 3–4) summarizes these decision roles.

MASTERY LEARNING

Conventional schooling is often criticized because of the large number of students who get lost along the way, students who show ability to learn what interests them outside school but who fail to learn what teachers require. Perhaps they feel that what they must learn in school is dull and irrelevant. Perhaps they fail to learn the fundamental concepts and skills and never catch up. Or they may have a few bad days—test days —and be labeled "slow learners." A skilled tutor could probably help them raise their performance, but tutors are prohibitively expensive, so these learners may be failed by their schools.

Mastery learning is an attempt to provide for all students some of the individualization of a tutorial approach without its heavy expense. Instruction based on a combination of mastery learning described by Block

(1971) and the Personalized System of Instruction described by Keller (1968) proceeds as follows. A teacher planning instruction first carefully defines the subject matter that students are to master and specifies questions that they should answer or skills that they should demonstrate as evidence of learning. Subject matter is then divided into small sequential units and a criterion test constructed for each unit. When a student feels adequately familiar with a unit, the criterion test is available. It requires a score of 80% or 90% correct for a "pass." Failure on the test requires the student to do some remedial study and then return to take a parallel form of the test. Passing the test is the ticket to the next unit. Lectures, demonstrations, and discussions are used primarily as reinforcers. For example, permission to attend the class of a popular teacher or to see a film is granted only when the student has completed certain unit tests. Alternatively, classes may be used as review sessions (punishment) for those having difficulty with unit tests.

Mastery learning uses tutoring in an important way. Each unit test is immediately graded by a proctor, who may be the teacher or a more advanced student. Immediate grading provides feedback and an opportunity for brief tutoring. When a student has completed the series of unit tests, the course is over and the grade is A. Lower grades come only as a consequence of failure to complete all units. The student is then eligible to start another course or perhaps an independent project, and such eligibility can in itself be highly reinforcing. An application of the Personalized System of Instruction in elementary school is described in Figure 3–1.

Figure 3–1. Personalized system of instruction (mastery learning) in second-grade spelling

KIDDIE PSI

by Tom Werner and Don McLaughlin
(The authors are graduate students
in psychology at West Virginia
University, Morgantown, W. Va.)

PSI has been transplanted intact from college to a second-grade spelling class at the Masontown, W. Va., elementary school. We believe that the program is unique for several reasons: (1) Students with minimal reading ability (our class consists of the slowest second-grade readers in the school) are being taught successfully by means of the written word; (2) Students work on their own, at their own rates, without the need for punishing deadlines; and (3) One day, when given the chance to vote, the class decided to do spelling rather than have recess. In addition, we believe we have the smallest course manager in PSI (3'6", 49 lbs).

Spelling class is held every morning for 20 minutes and students may work and take tests at various free times during the day. Our written material is the standard speller, which the class had previously used. The speller was already divided into units consisting of ten new spelling words and four pages of exercises. Before taking a unit test, the student must complete the exercises and have them certified to be 100% correct by a proctor. The proctor is one of the seven fastest students (in the class of 26) on that particular day.

The proctor then administers the test. The student must write nine of the ten spelling words correctly in order to pass. The student and the proctor then take the test to the course manager, who records the grade in the gradebook. The course manager is the student who was the most advanced during the previous week. If the student fails the test, the proctor helps the student to correct his mistakes and the student may re-take the test in a short while. After three unsuccessful attempts the student is proctored by the teacher.

Recently we instituted a token economy to encourage a higher rate of test-taking and a greater interest in proctoring. Students receive one token for correct wordbook exercises, one token for passing a unit, one token for proctoring, and two tokens for proctoring a student who is far behind.

PSI has produced numerous "rags to riches" stories in our classroom. One student completed what would have been one month's worth of spelling work in three days. Two students who had previously scored 20–30% on spelling tests have become top students and are two of our most dependable proctors. A student with a reported IQ score of 50 has exceeded the class's mean number of units passed.

One course manager took it upon himself to encourage slower students to take a test by offering his services to them as a proctor. One student whose permanent school record includes such comments as "behavior problem" and "this child will drive you crazy" is a regular proctor whose only remaining vice is the occasional pinching of the authors' rear ends. Our greatest challenge was a student who felt that we were the finest educators who ever lived for allowing him to go at his own pace . . . which he decided would be zero. After careful attention, prompting and indoctrination in the amenities of academia, he is now keeping up with the rest of the class. However, to this day, he suspects he was doublecrossed.

Although our course has not yet ended, present rates of unit completion indicate that nearly every student will master all 14 units in that speller. Preliminary data suggest that retention after two weeks is considerably better in the PSI format than in the traditional format.

In summary, all the benefits of PSI that have been reported in the literature dealing with college-level courses seem to have been enjoyed by our second-graders. The administration at Masontown has been receptive and supportive. We are encouraged by the results of our project and believe that elementary-level PSI should be expanded beyond this limited application. (Reprinted with permission from the authors and the *PSI Newsletter,* 1975, *3*(3), 1–6.)

ASSUMPTIONS ABOUT THE LEARNER

This strategy is not new to vocational and military training, but it has only recently appeared in "academic" settings. Implicit in mastery learning is a view of the learner that has heretofore unfortunately been absent in much of formal education. Mastery learning takes seriously the fact of individual differences among learners. The primary difference, however, is considered to be not aptitude, but the amount of time taken to master a learning task. This position implies that, given sufficient time and adequate instruction, most students can master most learning tasks (Carroll, 1963).

Mastery learning places responsibility for completing teacher-developed tasks directly on the learner. Because learning objectives are clearly specified and tests can be retaken, it is difficult to blame failure on poor instruction or on unfair tests. Little time need be spent trying to psych out the teacher or to devise ways of cheating. Failure on a unit test is likely to be the result of identifiable problems rather than of generalized "low ability." Mastery learning sees the learner as having considerable dignity. Keller puts it this way: "*The student is always right.* He is not asleep, not unmotivated, not sick, and he can learn a great deal if we provide the right contingencies of reinforcement" (1968, p. 88).

Mastery learning attempts to take the "course" as the unit of analysis and to provide the correct contingencies for effective learning. There is evidence from research, particularly in college settings, that these procedures do promote high retention of subject-matter knowledge and positive attitudes about a course. Small classroom groups and college courses of 1000 have experienced one or another version of mastery learning. Typically, two or three times as many A's are earned under mastery conditions as under traditional conditions. When compared with traditional instruction, mastery learning results in at least equivalent and often superior learning (on a common examination). Students experiencing mastery learning usually prefer it to traditional instruction, and some studies have shown that mastery-learning students develop more positive attitudes toward the subject matter (Block & Anderson, 1975; Kulik, Kulik, & Carmichael, 1974).

Mastery learning may also reduce competition among students for grades. Students attempt to improve their performance compared with their past performance, rather than to score higher on tests than other students do.

DECISION ROLES

What are the decision roles for teacher and learner when instruction is managed in this way? Mastery learning standardizes the objectives (content) of instruction and the evaluation criteria. But it individualizes the rate at which, and to some extent the procedures by which, learning occurs. The teacher remains very much in control, yet because learners may master the objectives at individual rates, slower learners may experience success nearly equal to that of fast learners.

Some educators fear that widespread use of mastery learning will result in A's for all students. That seems unlikely, although many more A's and many fewer failures do occur under mastery learning. The reduction of grade variability does not, however, eliminate all distinctions among learners, since differences remain in rate of learning. Under mastery learning some students finish faster than others, but each student is more likely to finish. Whether students earning A's do learn at the A standard may be easily determined by giving them an examination used previously when competitive grading was employed.

TEACHER-LEARNER CONTRACTS

A teacher-learner contract is an agreement between a learner and a teacher about the content and procedures of instruction.

Contracts may offset some of the disadvantages of mastery learning. Recall that mastery learning is sufficient for promoting the learning of well-defined subject matter and that students are generally more pleased with mastery learning than with conventional instruction. But mastery learning is not likely to promote certain important learning outcomes. It is unlikely to foster skill in choosing learning goals. It is unlikely to promote skills in self-evaluation. It is less appropriate for open-ended than for highly structured subject matter.

If students are to gain such skills as identifying significant problems, seeking relevant information and appraising their own progress, it may be useful to employ a more open, self-directed approach. Since students learn the method as well as the content of instruction, they must be treated as independent, resourceful learners if that is what they are to become. Such goals have implications for the teacher as well, for as the learner's role becomes more active, the teacher's role is likely to become more consultative. Indeed, the profession of consultant suggests this strategy—the contractual model. Let the teacher and learner negotiate services and obligations to their mutual satisfaction and state them in as formal a contract as they wish.

The contract may specify learning objectives, procedures for learning, mechanisms for evaluation, and/or some combination of these. One instructor in a college survey course prepares a list of objectives. She gives this "menu" to students to help them decide which objectives to pursue (Rogers, 1972). The selected objectives constitute a contract that reflects both teacher and student preference.

Suppose a student is undertaking an experience for personal growth, possibly an extended period of travel. Can that personal experience be turned into a bonafide educational experience? Events may be added to the itinerary that facilitate specific learning: interviewing experts in one's area of interest, speaking only the local language, capturing on film or tape a sociological portrait of the area. Since the fortuitous as well as the planned experiences of travel are highly educational, they too should be documented. To determine what has been learned fortuitously, however, requires a complete record of experience as well as considerable reflection. A journal may provide a helpful record. Describing the learning that has occurred may be difficult, yet that process of conceptualization is an essential aspect of the learning. A contract based on a travel experience, thus, might begin with a description of activities, and the learner's task might be to identify resultant learnings and to relate them to previous learning.

THE INTERPERSONAL DIMENSION
OF CONTRACTS

Teachers and students sometimes find it difficult to speak with each other about what and how they wish to learn. The stereotyped differences in authority between teachers and learners accent this reluctance. In this regard educators can learn from professionals in marriage and family counseling and in social psychiatry, who sometimes use contracts to formalize their transactions with clients. Their hope is to make interpersonal expectations explicit. "It is often difficult to get people to say openly and explicitly what they want and need from one another. . . . To reveal one's hand, so to speak, is often considered bad form because it may violate some social taboos or because it reduces the manipulative power of the revealer" (Shapiro, 1968, p. 172). In instruction as well as in therapy, negotiating a contract carries interpersonal expectations. Contracts may minimize a teacher's authoritarian tendencies ("You must learn it because it is good for you!") and increase the learner's initiative and responsibility. But to do so it is essential that the real payoff, the grade, also be negotiated or be under the control of the learner.

In a course for graduate students I attempted to use contracts as a way of placing students in control of objectives, procedures, and evaluation. I first provided some training in the writing of objectives. Students then constructed their own objectives for the course and gave a copy to me during the third week of the semester. At the end of the semester each student provided a grade based on evaluation of progress on those objectives. The other terms in the contract included at least three consultations with the instructor, completion of a journal describing significant learning experiences during the semester, and participation in an evaluation of the course. Student objectives ranged from personal behavior change (reduction of anxiety in social conversations) through work on classroom problems (constructing instructional material congruent with a particular theory of learning and testing the effectiveness of the materials) to traditional academic content (outlining similarities and differences between several theories of learning). Most students selected several objectives of varying types. No student failed, but a few dropped the course. Many provided self grades of B rather than A (Menges, 1972).

Not all contract strategies are so unstructured. Some learners respond poorly to the lack of structure that learner-initiated contracts imply. It may be necessary to increase learner autonomy gradually rather than to change as abruptly as I did in that course. Many teachers are uncomfortable in giving students the responsibility of deciding what they will learn and whether they have learned it. Therefore, particularly for younger children in school settings, teachers typically specify their roles in considerable detail. One discussion of contracts suggests that the teacher provide the student with the following as part of the contract:

1. An exact list of items that he must learn.
2. An exact method for showing the teacher that he has mastered the required learning.
3. A clear indication of how well he must do before he will be permitted to end one contract and begin another.
4. A choice of many media learning resources (tapes, records, films, books, pictures, single-concept loops, games, slides, etc.) on his academic level.
5. A choice of many activities through which information can be used and reinforced so that it becomes knowledge.
6. A choice of many ways in which he may share what he has learned with others (peers, teachers, younger or older children, etc.) [Dunn & Dunn, 1972, p. 79].

Even this rather limited notion of contract does individualize instruction. Learners move at different rates using different learning activities. They may also become more perceptive about their readiness to be examined on what they have learned. Teachers are less likely to lecture and to use other large-group methods and are more likely to treat students as individuals. Despite these advantages, it is doubtful that contracts in this form help students to become significantly more independent or self-directed, since the teacher decides what is to be learned and whether it has been learned.

DECISION ROLES

When the teacher manages instruction by using contracts, there are a number of possibilities for decision roles. Learners may be given virtually complete control, with the teacher retaining only the power of an ultimate veto, or learners and teachers may negotiate, or the teacher may specify everything. Most frequently, teachers reserve for themselves the tasks of setting objectives and making decisions about evaluation, while providing learners with choices about learning activities.

GAMES AND SIMULATIONS

A distinction is sometimes made between "learning" and "real learning." "We studied that in school last term," a student might say. "I guess I learned it then, but I didn't *really* learn it until I had to do it on my own at work over the weekend." The classroom and the world outside the classroom are seen as quite different; things are somehow more real outside the classroom.

There are two ways to merge the classroom with the world outside. One is to move learning out of the classroom, and the next section of this chapter describes "total immersion," a strategy for doing just that. The other is to introduce reality into the classroom, and games and simulations are devices for approximating reality in a classroom context.

Games and simulations are not synonymous. A game has explicit rules that constrain the interaction of players. The rules are particular to that game and lead to a predetermined end point. Simulations are models of reality, but are always limited and simplified representations. In a simulation players interact in ways somewhat like the ways they would interact in reality. "Poker, for example, is an ordinary game in that it is not a model of some other, non-game activity; Monopoly, on the other hand, is a simulation of the real estate business—albeit a poor one" (Zuckerman & Horn, 1973, p. 1).

Hundreds of games and simulations have been developed, and many are commercially available. One of them simulates establishing and maintaining a social order and is called "SIMSOC, Simulated Society." Another, "Democracy," represents the legislative process in the United

States. Others deal with language skills, business, math, and virtually all other topics studied in school. Three examples are described in Figure 3–2. Two of them provide specific problem-solving situations, one in ecological policy and the other in educational policy. The third is aimed at creating new program ideas for use in a youth organization. Curriculum units incorporating games and simulations are also available. They may include materials for weeks or even months of activity and be structured around objectives that are part of the conventional school curriculum. There is even a simulation, "Jabberwockey," in which participants create simulations.

Figure 3–2. Examples of games and simulations

Dirty Water

Aimed at grades four through high school, this game is played by two to four players for an hour or two. Players assume such roles as City Administrator of Water Quality. Using a game board, dice, and cards, they make decisions related to water pollution and population control with the aim of stocking and maintaining an ecologically balanced lake and an appropriate population size. Although dice determine many events randomly, there is opportunity for both conflicting and cooperative interaction among players. The game is meant to teach about both ecology and the decision-making process. A pretest and posttest are available (Anderson et al., 1970).

Participative Decision Making

This exercise has three purposes: to introduce the topic of program budgeting to nonprofessionals and professionals in education, to introduce the process of participative decision making, and to demonstrate a simulation for persons attending a conference. The unlimited number of participants may be high school age or older and spend two to four hours with the exercise. Persons in the role of taxpayer, parent, student, teacher, principal, and school-board member are presented with the need to cut the school budget for the next year. Consequent interaction reveals the implict educational priorities of players and the intricacies of decision making (Horn, 1970).

Impact: A Youth-Ministry Simulation

Up to 60 persons in teams of 6 to 8 may spend from three hours to one day engaged in this simulation. Through interaction, the players of junior-high age and up attempt to formulate and carry out a youth-ministry strategy appropriate to their own town. Players take roles of youth advisors, youth group members, and uncommitted youth. New ideas for strategies and programs are generated from participants' interactions (Shukraft & Washburn, 1970).

In each of the examples in Figure 3–2, participants act as if the situation were real. Since the activity is only a representation of reality, each participant is protected from the anxieties and risks inherent in real-world events. Thus it is possible to examine options and to take chances that one might not ordinarily take. In each example there is opportunity for individuals to demonstrate skills. Chance plays a role too, as it does in reality, but an effective simulation never permits chance to be the controlling factor. A good game or simulation also provides considerable interaction. Participants may get a new perspective on how they deal with tension and conflict because of feedback from other players. Finally, participation includes an opportunity for reflection. This period after play is usually called "debriefing" and enables participants to consider what they did as players and what it means. Since there is usually considerable variety in interpretation from one participant to another, debriefing is often as stimulating as playing itself.

THE PROCESS OF LEARNING FROM EXPERIENCE

Educators have tried to explain the nature of the learning processes involved in learning from such experiences as games and simulations. A four-step sequence was suggested (J. S. Coleman et al., 1973). (1) Action. The player makes a move and notes its consequences. (2) Understanding the particular case. The player identifies the particular circumstances under which the same consequence would follow from a move in the future. (3) Generalizing. The player identifies a range of circumstances under which the same consequence occurs (identifies a principle). (4) Acting in a new circumstance. The player puts the knowledge to use in a different but generalizable situation.

This process of experiential learning is quite different from the steps involved in information processing, the sort of learning that results from, say, mastery learning. In information processing, one first receives information, then understands, and finally acts. (Note that action is the final step in both types of learning.) But action, applying the principle in a new situation, very seldom occurs in conventional instruction except in an artificial context such as a test. Therefore one may report "learning, but not *real* learning." On the other hand, action is almost certain to occur in an effective game or simulation, because participation requires active decision making.

Experiential learning is undoubtedly very important. But it is expensive in time and effort and it is probably not the most efficient way to teach subject matter. Research shows that participants in games and simulations typically learn as much subject matter as students in regular classes, but that they seldom learn more and take longer to acquire what they do learn. For content learning, lectures and texts are probably more efficient. If the teacher is seeking to motivate students, however, games and simulations may be helpful, for they do involve students more actively in the learning process. If attitudes are considered an important outcome, games and simulations may also be recommended. Students report liking them and often show more positive attitudes toward the subject matter involved. They may also show more accepting attitudes to the real life counterpart of the role they have played, for example, the role of a person from a different social class or ethnic background. Some of these benefits are greater for students of high ability than for those of low ability. The latter seem to learn the skills that are instrumental for winning and seem to be interested, but they have difficulty applying their learning beyond the game or simulation, probably because application requires understanding the analogies between the activity and its real-life counterpart (J. S. Coleman et al., 1973; Wentworth & Lewis, 1973).

DECISION ROLES

In games and simulations, learners are involved in a special way. They are decision makers. The teacher selects the strategy and thereby determines learning objectives. But a game or simulation requires active participation by learners, so the learner has considerable influence on the direction learning takes. The learner also has a role in evaluation, since much of experiential learning is personal. The teacher can make a formal appraisal, of course, but must trust the learner to integrate some learning privately. In short, while the teacher chooses the vehicle for learning, it is the learner who affects the development of the learning experience and who ultimately assesses its effectiveness.

TOTAL IMMERSION

Dr. John R. Coleman has been a professor at the Massachusetts Institute of Technology, staff member of the Ford Foundation, Chairman of the Board of the Federal Reserve Bank in Philadelphia, and President of Haverford College. As a college president, he sometimes advised students to take a break from study, perhaps to change the rhythm of their lives by working in some setting very different from a classroom.

In 1973, when he was 51 years old, President Coleman requested a leave of absence in order to follow his own advice. Telling no one the details of his plans, he set out in his car to experience the world of the laborer. He took along a little cash, some books, and the help-wanted ads.

Atlanta provided work in sewer construction, mostly ditch-digging. It was heavy work, and Atlanta is sometimes cold in February. As the days passed, Coleman's body grew stronger and his psyche adjusted to the jibes of his boss, Gus: "The trouble with you guys is you're all ironheads. You don't think. You use your muscles and your feet when you should use your heads" (J. R. Coleman, 1974, p. 38).

Later, in Boston, he spent several weeks as a sandwich man at the Union Oyster House. He was there long enough to feel himself growing into the job, becoming skillful and feeling pride in his skills. He knew for sure that he was admitted to the elite circle of employees the day the cook gave him fish for lunch. Twice before he had asked for fish but received the employee's menu instead. "But today I thought I'd try asking again. It worked. Giving me the scrod was Jacob's way of taking me into the circle" (J. R. Coleman, 1974, p. 176).

When he quit that job—he had to chair a meeting of bank directors in Philadelphia the next day—he was tremendously pleased that his work had been "more than just satisfactory." If he ever looked for work in Boston again, the boss said in parting, he should try the Oyster House.

Upon first arriving in Boston, he had tried a porter-dishwasher job in another eatery, a cafeteria. He had been on the job about an hour when the boss handed him two dollars. "This isn't your work, I can tell." Being fired for no discernible reason had left him low. He left the Oyster House as high as he had been low when fired a few weeks earlier.

In Maryland he worked as a trash collector and took pride in that, too. When one woman, angry that his crew could not take her cinder blocks, said "Who are you to say what goes? You're nothing but a trashman," Coleman shared the embarrassment of crew members as well as their defensive pride (J. R. Coleman, 1974, p. 222). The following Sunday afternoon, dressed in a suit, he drove through the same neighborhood. Just because he was a well-dressed driver, he found that residents' smiles replaced cold stares given to the trashmen.

Coleman's courageous experiment illustrates a powerful educational tool: learning about something new and unfamiliar by totally immersing oneself in it.

Apprenticeships, medical internships, student teaching, and campus-orientation visits all employ this procedure in a limited way; all represent a kind of partial immersion. A high school student named Robin participated in one such internship, designed as a low-risk introduction to work situations:

> Robin hasn't missed a single day in court since she started working with a judge in a Kansas county courthouse. This serious sixteen year old "shadows" the judge as he prepares cases. She sits in when he confers with jurors, attorneys and officials of the court. She has been so

attentive that the judge assigned her a special project of her own. She is to research the legality of adult adoption in the manner of a law clerk. "Robin doesn't do any filing or secretarial work," comments the judge. "The important thing for her is to get insight into the experiences of the courts" [Resources for Youth, 1975, p. 1].

The teacher in training is given partial responsibility for real students in a real school. Everyone knows, of course, that the student teacher is there only temporarily and that real authority (the power of discipline and grades) is held by others. Nevertheless, the student teacher learns a great deal about what teaching is like, and more than one has decided at that point either to deepen a commitment to teaching or to move toward a different profession. In medical education, a student is sometimes assigned to a particular family during medical-school years. The student is responsible for their medical care and thus feels considerably more personal responsibility than does a student teacher charged with perhaps 100 students. In addition to learning something of what medical practice is like, the student is accountable under supervision for advising and treating his or her family.

The internship immerses the learner in a long-term, semiprotected training situation. To have maximum impact, however, immersion should be total. Ties to conventional roles and activities must be cut so that one is known only in terms of the new environment. One must change identity and be thrown on one's own resources. That is what President Coleman did by plunging into the world of the laborer. As we learn in the following sections, others have plunged into inner-city environments or outdoor-survival experiences.

TAKING THE PLUNGE IN CHICAGO

Since 1964 the Urban Training Center in Chicago has offered a four-week orientation on the problems of urban society. After a few days of general sessions, trainees are expected to take the "plunge." They move anonymously into the city's life with only a few dollars for each of the three or four days they will live there. Their normal roles are social worker or teacher or minister; now they become members of the underclass, clients of those same professional roles. They stay at a skid-row mission and try to get a day's work in an employment line at 5 A.M. If they try to warm up in a restaurant, sleep in a movie theater, or ask too aggressively for a job, they may hear the threat "Move along or I'll call the police."

One trainee who happened to be a minister approached a clerically garbed man in a restaurant. The trainee asked politely about a pin the other wore. "Well," said the cleric, enunciating as if he were in his pulpit, "I am a clergyman of this city and this pin shows a fish, signifying that I am a fisher of men."

The trainee spoke about his hard times and his need for a job. "I don't know where I can sleep tonight. Please, how can I get some work?"

"Well, son, tomorrow night is prayer meeting at our church. You should come. I would like to see you there." So much for fishers of men, concluded the trainee.

On the plunge, trainees experience the utter inhumanity of city life for the poor. They are viewed with suspicion and hostility by ordinary citizens and victimized and exploited by the very agencies established to serve them. Trainees who themselves grew up in poverty weep to rediscover the desperation of those experiences. Time softens such memories; the plunge brings them back forcefully.

The plunge causes the trainee's values to be "seen in high relief," according to Father Morton, Urban Training Center's former director. It serves as a reference point during the rest of the orientation program when trainees plan specific proposals for change in their jobs back home.

TAKING THE WILDERNESS SOLO

The Outward Bound Schools offer a three- to four-week training program that includes a wilderness solo-survival experience. Students spend approximately three days and three nights isolated in a wilderness location, supplied only with the clothes they wear, six matches, and a six-foot-square waterproof cloth. Students, typically 16 to 21 years of age, regard the experience as an initiation, an endurance test. The solo is also intended as a time for reflection, a time for becoming closer to oneself. A description of part of one solo follows (written by a person somewhat older than most).

> My solo site was a beautiful island in the middle of a secluded lake, several days by canoe from people. The clear, bright air made it all magical. I bathed in this idyllic atmosphere, then I bathed in the smooth, crystal waters. Then I became serious. The wilderness expert emerged; the child of nature vanished. The shelter was constructed, the wood pile collected, and the fire started—with one match. And there I sat. During the next three days and nights my shelter and my fire became very important parts of my world. I had no idea how important they would become that first sun-filled afternoon.
>
> But the night changed things. The night was long and hard to get through. It was cold. The wood pile became small so quickly. As the fire burned down to white coals, the cold air brought me out of my shelter, and I built the fire back into flames. I stayed by the flames for a while, and got warmed up. Sitting there, lit up by the flames in the

dark silence, I felt completely alone, but not lonely. I realized that information about myself was now emerging in bold relief. There were no other persons or institutions around to confuse the issue, no convenient way to project feelings on others or lay blame on an institution. In the uncomplicated environment of the solo, my thoughts and actions paraded about, expressing me in an obvious fashion. If I decided to order my day in the usual manner, this would be me "speaking," me seeking a certain kind of order in my existence. The solo could be an unusual chance to observe myself and gain some understanding, provided, of course, I could refrain from projecting, and, in fact, confront myself. That was not so easy to do [Katz, 1969, pp. 41–42].

The students are not objectively entirely alone, since they can be contacted or can contact others in case of emergency. What is important is the subjective sense of aloneness. The challenge is to go beyond the endurance aspect, "getting through the solo," to new awareness and new perceptions. The successful solo involves appreciation of such changes as a new sense of time and different sleep patterns. These changes are seen not as disruptive, but as a hint of the order of the wilderness, an order that transcends the individual.

The strategy of total immersion has also been integrated into programs of formal education. College students have received credit for taking an urban plunge into Boston's inner city. Outward Bound has designed wilderness experiences and offered them as courses in a number of high schools and colleges. Educators and students agree that total immersion is a powerful experience.

What is learned from these experiences? How do they relate to the goals of schooling? Information learning, in the sense of school subject matter, seems not to be a major outcome of total immersion. More obvious and dramatic outcomes are those resulting from physical stress and the mental challenge of confronting new and strange experiences. President Coleman indicated that he wished to test his muscles as well as his perceptions; Outward Bound students also test their physical limits. Coleman had realized that the top person, the president or the chairman, is in contact primarily with people who share his or her values, and he wished to identify with others from whom he felt cut off. For students on an urban plunge there is contact with persons from very different backgrounds. In an Outward Bound course, there are fellow students from a variety of places, holding a variety of values, now thrown close together.

Yet among the confusion of experiences, one does acquire a great deal of information and may spend weeks trying to sort out the bombardment of stimulation. Heightened motivation produced by these experiences may cause learners to be more receptive to related subject-matter instruction when it occurs subsequently in the classroom.

DECISION ROLES

Compared with the other teaching/learning strategies discussed in this chapter, total immersion introduces a new kind of teacher: the environment. The human teacher and the environment-as-teacher together decide what is to be learned. Once a learner is immersed in that environment, the human teacher has no direct influence. It is the learner in interaction with the planned environment that results in learning. Much of the resulting learning is private, never to be known to the teacher. The learner must reflect on the adequacy of the learning. The teacher may know what the student did, yet remain unaware of the significance of those actions to the student. In this sense, total immersion gives a very important evaluative role to the learner.

Using total immersion, the teacher as manager selects an environment that is likely to provide desirable learning. The environment is real, not artificial, as in a classroom, so it produces "real" learning. The teacher may assist the learner to deal with this highly charged learning, but must trust the learner's appraisal of its significance. The teacher decides what is to be learned; the learner in interaction with the environment decides how the learning takes place; and the learner in consultation with the teacher decides the significance of the learning.

LEARNERS AS TEACHERS

The most important stimulus to learning in everyday situations is probably interaction with one's fellow workers, fellow students, friends, and family members. Faced with a common task or a common problem to solve, peers naturally cooperate and learn from one another. Yet in classrooms the frequency of cooperative activities is not high, because of the competitive nature of much formal instruction. Most teachers nevertheless profess cooperation as one of their goals, and many teachers attempt to reward cooperation when it occurs.

One way to make cooperation occur more frequently is to have students teach other students. This seems especially important where there are tensions, such as racial tensions, that alienate certain students. Consider what happened to Carlos. He was seldom called on and never volunteered in his fifth-grade classroom. Then a team of psychologist-consultants changed the classroom rules, and Carlos could no longer be withdrawn. In order to set a norm of cooperation, they turned learning into a jigsaw puzzle and gave each student one piece. In a lesson on Joseph Pulitzer, for example, a six-paragraph biography was available. Pupils were divided into groups of six, and each child was given one paragraph. The child was expected to master that paragraph and to teach it to other group members as they jointly prepared for a test. Any pupil who needed help could consult with the member in another group who had the same paragraph. At first Carlos found teaching others difficult and was uncomfortable. Some other children realized that their only chance to do well on the test was to listen and to learn from Carlos. Some teased him, but others gave him respect and attention. Carlos relaxed. The others began to see him as not so dumb as they had thought, and friendships began to develop. As part of their research findings, the consultants concluded that these jigsaw-puzzle students learned as much as or more than comparison students and that their positive feelings for classmates increased (Aronson, 1975).

Note that in this example the teacher retained responsibility for evaluating student learning. In fact, one unfortunate outcome of such a strategy may be that students cooperate only out of self-defense against the test or against the teacher. A somewhat different approach is illustrated by one of the teaching styles described in Mosston's book. It is called "Reciprocity" and fosters cooperation in part by giving learners some responsibility for evaluating their own learning. Each small group of students is given a particular task—for example, a tumbling exercise in a physical education class. Each learner takes a turn as the "doer" while others serve as the "teacher-partners." While the doer tumbles, each teacher-partner observes. One observer might watch head movements, another watch leg movements, and so on. Then they provide feedback to the doer, who tries again. In this case the teacher-partners may have the responsibility of deciding when the doer has satisfactorily mastered the task. The teacher reinforces that role by never communicating directly with the doer, only with the teacher-partners (Mosston, 1972). This strategy may be adaptable for creative-writing tasks, math problems, or social-science projects.

As students learn together, they gain skills in identifying worthwhile questions as well as skills in finding answers. An entire university curriculum based on learning cells has been proposed and illustrates such cooperative learning. According to this proposal, learning cells are formed with membership equal to the number of courses each student in the cell is taking (probably four or five). Each member then teaches one subject to the others in the cell. Faculty prepare bibliographies and specify minimum standards. Questions not resolved by the cell members are taken up in a weekly tutorial with the professor and graduate teaching assistant who are also available during specified office hours. A final examination is supervised by the professor and covers only the relatively permanent fundamentals of the discipline. Preferably, exams are open book or oral in format, with at least half of the questions written by students. The questions as well as the answers are graded. With the exception of acquiring certain skills (for example, speaking a foreign language or operating an electron microscope) and learning about problems on the relatively unstructured frontiers of knowledge, this strategy could apply to a great deal of the school and college curriculum. The originator of this learning-cells proposal asserts "The best way for a student to learn a well-defined and recorded body of knowledge is to teach it to another" (Ackoff, 1968, p. B 123).

TUTORING AMONG UNEQUALS

So far we have assumed that students, equally unfamiliar with subject matter, are learning together. Each learns and then shares that learning. But much teaching by learners involves those who are more advanced and perhaps older teaching others who are less advanced and perhaps younger. One large-scale, community-based, government-funded project took place in Roane County, Tennessee. High school students there volunteered as much as 1600 hours in one month. (That is the equivalent of 13 full-time teachers.) The students act as individual tutors to elementary or junior high students, particularly in reading and math (Hartman, 1975).

Some students communicate more effectively with other students than do some teachers. Tutoring is emotionally rewarding to these students, who believe that they learn a great deal by teaching others. Yet those who volunteer to tutor are not miniature professional teachers. One study compared tutor volunteers with undergraduates in teacher education and found the tutors to have lower needs for deference, order, and endurance and a higher need for autonomy (Cox & Patton, 1970). Since tutors function under less structure than teachers, those differences seem appropriate. Persons being tutored probably respond more warmly to the less authoritarian tutor, and that warmth may enhance the tutor's sense of autonomy.

Research on age differences among tutors is discussed by Good and Brophy (1973). Elementary-age tutors were found to be direct and business-like, whereas those of college age were more indirect. The latter seemed to be seeking friendship as well as specific learning outcomes and often got involved in tangential matters with the persons they were tutoring. Despite these differences, research suggests that both older and younger tutors can be effective.

In a study of sixth-graders tutoring younger children, Powell (1975) learned that tutors tended to copy what their teachers did, including activities, such as drill, that the tutors themselves disliked. They could not use creative teaching procedures until such procedures had been modeled for them. Powell identified six stages that these tutors went through as they gained experience: (1) First, tutors assume a teacher-like role to establish their authority and sense of competence. (2) Next, they begin to identify the needs and interests of their pupils. (3) Then they find or create materials appropriate for the child's interests. (4) After pursuing that activity for a time, tutors learn to sense when it has lost its usefulness. (5) By this time the child is reinforcing the tutor and they are each confirming the other's expectations. (6) Finally, tutors become reflective as they begin to see effects on themselves from the tutoring. They become both more self-critical and more comfortable in the role of tutor.

These stages seem similar to those that many teachers experience with a new group of students. The stages are helpful for new tutors or supervisors of tutors to keep in mind. A supervisor can check a tutor's knowledge of the students' needs, for example, and the degree to which activities specific to those needs are developed (Stages 2 and 3). Evaluations written after each tutoring session can chart progress over time and clarify when it is time to change activities (Stage 4). Tutors meeting together can reflect on the personal values of their experiences (Stage 6).

A TRIANGLE OF OUTCOMES

What are the benefits of learners acting as teachers? Three learning outcomes can be visualized as the points in a triangle: cognitive growth for the learner, cognitive growth for the tutor, and interpersonal benefits. Klaus (1975) suggests that a given program is likely to be successful with one or perhaps two of these outcomes, but unlikely to be successful with all three.

If cognitive growth of the *learner* is the aim, a highly structured program is most effective. Using drill and repetition, the tutor becomes almost a human teaching machine. But such an approach may result in narrow learning not well integrated with the school curriculum.

If a program aims at academic gains for the *tutor,* the tutor must be given opportunities to identify needs, plan activities, and appraise results. Unfortunately the child's learning is not guaranteed by the tutor's learning. The learning cells described by Ackoff may be a less risky setting for this goal than a setting in which older children tutor younger ones.

Interpersonal learning is facilitated, reasonably enough, when subject matter is deemphasized and social skills are taught. These skills include focusing on the learner's strengths, giving negative feedback in a constructive way, and showing empathy. (Empathy is discussed in the next chapter.) Klaus's discussion implies that teachers need to be conscious of the outcomes they seek when encouraging learners to be teachers. Only then can they choose appropriate procedures for implementation.

DECISION ROLES

Now let us review the decision roles that exist when a teacher as manager employs the strategy of learners as teachers. Who decides what is to be learned? The teacher does—but remember that the "teacher" may be a learner who has temporarily assumed a tutoring role. Who decides on learning activities? Again it is the teacher (tutor), perhaps in collaboration with the learner (tutee). Who decides when learning is satisfactorily completed? Probably the adult teacher does, since grading is a responsibility dear to most teachers. Nevertheless, the tutor may provide the teacher with information essential for making that evaluation.

Even at its most limited, this strategy demonstrates that persons other than teachers are significant learning resources and that learning in cooperation with others can benefit all.

LEARNING NETWORKS

Many activities learners consider most important for promoting learning are almost incidental to the schools' main functions. These include meeting other people who are interested in the same things, learning something they always thought would be fun to know, and sharing what they know with others who want to learn. Suppose there were a service that connects a person who wants to learn something with another person who wants to teach it. Such a service is a learning network.

Here are some things one learning network has done. A woman received a cuckoo clock from Germany accompanied by instructions in German. Since she reads no German, she relied on the service to find a translator and subsequently took German lessons from this retired German teacher. A high school girl teaches the flute to a group of adults twice her age. A student is tutored in French free in return for weeding the tutor's garden.

The Learning Exchange in Evanston, Illinois, was started in 1971 and is really just an arrangement for bringing people together. Its files contain 13,000 teachers and learners, and the annual catalog lists over 2600 topics. Someone who wishes to teach, to learn, or to share an interest calls The Learning Exchange. Files are searched, resulting in a list of names and phone numbers of people who match the caller's interests. The caller gets in touch with them, and together they decide when, where, and how often to meet, what resources are necessary, whether or not there will be a fee, and so on. About half the teachers charge a fee, usually based on ability to pay. There are no grades, degrees, certificates, classrooms, tuition, requirements, or competition.

The Learning Exchange in Evanston was founded by Denis Detzel and Robert Lewis, then graduate students at Northwestern University. They were influenced by the ideas of Ivan Illich, who is highly critical of schooling systems and particularly of their emphasis on credentials. Illich wants people to take responsibility for their own learning rather than to transfer that responsibility to institutions. For him, the important learning-resource persons are not a professionally trained elite, but anyone with appropriate knowledge, skills, experience, and the motivation to share.

A network of teachers and learners is one of Illich's suggestions in his book *Deschooling Society* (1971), and The Learning Exchange is a switchboard for such a network. The pages reproduced from The Learning Exchange catalog (Figure 3–3) illustrate the range of its offerings. According to an Exchange newsletter, one may learn how to repair a Volkswagen (fix a bug) or learn self-defense using Kung Fu (foil a thug). One may learn to play conventional or exotic musical instruments (play a tune) or discuss and perhaps create new living arrangements (join a commune).

While most offerings are practical or deal with theory in the context of practice, others are primarily theoretical—for example, examinations of structuralism, political philosophy, Piaget and education, or the books of Norman O. Brown and Carlos Castaneda.

Another program of The Learning Exchange is the "telephone encyclopedia." Persons willing to answer questions by telephone on a particular topic may list themselves and their interest. Callers are referred to them when they have a question on that topic, and their only obligation is to answer questions by phone.

Why do people participate in The Learning Exchange? Not to gain credit or grades or certificates. Not to earn money. But because it matters to them, because learning or teaching serves *their* purposes. The Learning Exchange is a service controlled by the participants, not by an institution.

DECISION ROLES

The Learning Exchange is the last teaching/learning strategy considered in this chapter. And it is the clearest example of learner control. Nothing happens at The Learning Exchange without learners who identify something they wish to learn, arrange resources (human and otherwise) to help themselves learn, and decide when their learning is of sufficient quality and quantity that their experience should be terminated. It is the learner's initiative that makes The Learning Exchange work.

A learning network has two great benefits. One is that learners gain what they set out to learn. The other is the self-knowledge acquired,

For each topic on this list, at least one person was registered to teach, learn, and/or share their interest in that subject as of May 1974. If you don't see what you're looking for on this list, just give us a call. We may already have somebody on file who listed themselves after this catalog was printed. We'll also be happy to list you under the topic(s) you're interested in so that future callers will be referred to you.

Occupational Therapy
Ocean-going Vessels
Oceanography
Office Filing Methods
Office Procedures
Office Work
Offset Printing
Ombudsmen, Urban
Ontology
Opera
Oral Interpretation
Orchestra
Organ
  Electric
  Pipe
  Portative & Positive
Organ (Theatre) Restoration
Organic Foods Co-ops
Organic Foods
Organic Gardening
Organizational Skills
Orgones
Orientation
Origami
Orphanage, Experimental
Oud
Outdoor Skills
Overseas Correspondence

P

PERT—Program Evaluation & Review Technique
Pacifism
Package Design
Paddleball
Paddle Tennis
Paganism
Painting
  Acrylic
  Airbrush
  Japanese Brush
  Oil
  Watercolor
  Watercolor for Children
Painting Estimating
Painting, House *Indoor & Outdoor*
Painting, Restoration
Pa-Kua
Paleontology
Palm Reading
Pantomime
Papal Audiences
Paper Tole
Paramedical Careers

Paranormal Learning in Children
Parapsychology
Parent Education
Parent Power
Parents' Effectiveness Training (P.E.T.)
Parliamentary Procedure
Paste-up (Keyline)
Pastoral Theology
Pastry Work
Patents
Patient Power
Pattern Making
Peace
Pentecostal Movement
People's Yellow Pages
Perceptually Handicapped
Percussion Instruments
Perls, Fritz
Persia & Persian Culture
Persian
Personal Growth & Development
Personality Testing
Personnel Management
Pest Control
Pharmacology
Philippine Dialect
Philosophy
  Chakra
  Discussion Group
  Eastern
  Ethics
  Existentialism
  Freedom & Spiritual Action
  Indian
  Kierkegaard
  Mental
  Nineteenth Century
  Occult
  Of Religion
  Sartre, Jean-Paul
  Steiner, Rudolph
  Schweitzer, Albert
  Value of Violence
  Western
Phonetics
Phonics
Photographic History
Photography *All aspects*
  Career Information-especially freelance
  Clubs
  Commercial
  Creative
  Darkroom
  Exhibiting

Lighting
Nature
Racing
Schilleran
Theory
Photojournalism
Photomicrography
Photo Silkscreening
Physical Education
Physical Science
Physical Therapy
Physics
Physiology
Piano *All types & levels*
Piano Rebuilding, Repair & Refinishing
Piano Tuning
Picnic Table Construction
Picture Framing
Ping Pong
Pinochle
Pipe Organ
Pipe Organ Building
Pizza Making
Plants (Indoor)
Plastering
Plaster Molds
Plastics
Plate Collecting, Limited Edition
PLATO (Urbana Base Computer Instruction System)
Plays
  Production
  Reading
  Twentieth Century
  Writing
Plexiglass Construction
Plumbing
Plunger Arts
Poetry
  Analysis
  Contemporary
  Contemporary American
  Humorous
  Readings
  Writing
  Workshop
Poker
Police Chemistry
Police-Community Problems
Police Reform
Polish
Polish Military History
Political Organizing (Boycotts)
Political Science
  European
  Far East
  General
Political Theory
Political Theory, Radical
Politics
  American
  Current
  Independent
  People's Party

Practical
Polka
Polka Musicians
Pollution
Polo
Polydomes
Polynesia
Pool
Popular Culture
Population
Portraiture
Portuguese
Positive Mental Attitude
Postcard Collecting
Postcards
Pottery
  Apprenticeship
  Ceramics
  Kiln Space
Pregnancy Testing
Preschool Education
Priceless Society
Primal Therapy
Printing
  Management & Production
  Offset
Print Making
Prisons
  Bail
  Counseling
  Reform
  Visitations
Private Investigation
Problem Solving (Individual)
Process—Church of the Final Judgement
Production Management
Proofreading
Prose Poetry
Psychiatric Rehabilitation
Psychiatrists, Problems with
Psychiatry Racket
Psychic Development
Psychic Phenomena
Psychic Readings
Psychic Research
Psychic Sciences
Psychoanalysis
Psycho-Cybernetics
Psychodrama
Psychological Testing
Psychologists, Problems with
Psychology
  Adler, Alfred
  Child
  Clinical Personality
  Counseling
  Creative
  Crime and Personality
  Integration
  General
  Horney, Karen
  Humanistic
  Personality Theory
  Responsibility & Will

24

25

Figure 3–3. Pages from The Learning Exchange catalog

knowledge about the learner's own needs, learning styles and processes, and incentives and rewards.

The Learning Exchange may seem incompatible with the constraints of school classrooms, but limited experimentation in schools is by no means impossible. A teacher in the role of manager might encourage a student-initiated network within a school. Part of two afternoons a week could be devoted to teacher-learner contact. This is "learners as teachers" with a twist: participation is wholly voluntary, and content is not in the service of the official school curriculum. Such learning and teaching should be fun and it should be self-fulfilling.

A society such as ours requires institutions that grade and sort and certify people for the economic marketplace. Schools have served and will continue to serve that function. Sadly, as schools pursue those tasks, they make learning sometimes tedious, usually competitive, and often fraught with anxiety. A learning network promotes learning and teaching, not grading and credentialing. Networks will never replace schools, but they can serve as alternatives and even as inspirations to teachers and to schools.

DECISION MAKING AND THE TEACHER AS MANAGER

The teacher as manager is concerned with decisions about instructional goals, activities, and criteria. As manager, the teacher places more emphasis on subject-matter learning than on specific observable behaviors (as in the controller role) or on feelings and emotions (as in the helper role).

The fundamental management decision defines the relative roles of teacher and learner. To what extent is the teacher *vis-à-vis* the learner to choose objectives, activities, and evaluation criteria? Depending on the answer to this question and generally on the instructional goals, the manager chooses a particular teaching/learning strategy from a variety of possible strategies. Six strategies are described in this chapter. They are listed in Figure 3–4 along with an indication of the teacher/learner decision role appropriate to each. This chart should assist teachers in making management decisions appropriate to the intended relationship between learner and teacher.

Choice of a strategy will reflect the teacher's feelings and values as well as knowledge. One very relevant feeling dimension is trust, and the strategies range widely on this dimension. In mastery learning, for example, learners need be trusted for very little, since they regulate only their rate of learning. In a learners-as-teachers strategy the teacher must trust students (1) to be interested in the teaching/learning process and (2) to

Figure 3-4. Decision roles for six teaching/learning strategies

Strategy	Who decides . . .		
	what is learned?	how it is learned?	when it has been learned?
Mastery learning	Teacher	Teacher, possibly learner	Teacher
Teacher-learner contracts	Teacher, perhaps learner	Teacher, perhaps learner	Teacher, possibly learner
Games and simulations	Teacher	Teacher and learner	Teacher and learner
Total immersion	Teacher	Environment and learner	Learner, possibly teacher
Learners as teachers	Teacher, learner as teacher	Teacher, learner as teacher	Teacher, learner as teacher
Learning network	Learner	Learner, together with teacher	Learner

trust other learners as resources for learning. In a learning network, learners must not only be trusted by teachers but also have a great deal of trust in themselves.

To make good decisions as managers, teachers must be informed about available strategies and must also be in touch with their own feelings. In the next chapter, we turn to the topic of feelings and emotions.

FOR FURTHER READING

The spectrum of seven teaching styles described by Mosston (1972) examines in much more detail some of the issues raised in the introduction to this chapter. Mosston subtitles his book "From Command to Discovery," suggesting that the spectrum ranges from one extreme at which the teacher is entirely in charge (command) to the other extreme at which the learner is in charge (discovery). For discussions of other teaching/learning strategies, see *Practical Approaches to Individualizing Instruction* (Dunn & Dunn, 1972) and *Educational Innovator's Guide* (Von Haden & King, 1974).

An important managerial function of teachers involves testing students, either to assign them to appropriate learning experiences or to assess their learning after instruction. The use of standardized tests is described in *Standardized Testing in the Schools: Uses and Roles* (Wardrop, 1975). *Educational Measurement: Where Are We Going and How Will We Know When We Get There?* (Wick, 1973) provides suggestions for planning and grading classroom tests.

Mastery Learning

This discussion of mastery learning does not distinguish among several instructional plans that share a concern for mastery. One, described in *Mastery Learning: Theory and Practice* (Block, 1971), is likely to use unit tests more for diagnosis than for grading. It is also likely to employ group-based classroom procedures. Another major approach is the Personalized System of Instruction (PSI) originated by behavioral psychologist Fred Keller. PSI is more widely used in higher education than with younger students and is described by Keller (1968), Ruskin (1974), and Ryan (1974). Both approaches share a concern for individualization, sequential mastery, feedback, and tutorial assistance.

Current research and materials on the Personalized System of Instruction are available from the Center for Personalized Instruction, Georgetown University, Washington, D.C. 20027.

Good sources of practical suggestions on organizing a mastery-learning course are the small books by Block and Anderson (1975) and Ryan (1974).

Teacher-Learner Contracts

A comprehensive description of the contract approach, including detailed examples, is in Chapter Three of *Practical Approaches to Individualizing Instruction* (Dunn & Dunn, 1972).

Some elements of learning contracts for college students are discussed in a collection of articles on individualizing instruction edited by Berte (1975).

A very helpful book for learning to state specific instructional objectives (for oneself or others) is *Preparing Instructional Objectives* (Mager, 1962).

Games and Simulations

Simulating a society in a classroom may seem impractical, but one excellent effort to have students experience an economically based society in their school ("a real world in miniature") is described in *The Micro-Society School* (Richmond, 1973). Richmond's work also documents an urban school system's resistance to innovation.

Two journals concerned with describing and researching this teaching/learning strategy are *Simulation/Gaming/News* and *Simulation and Games.*

Catalogs of exercises, games, and simulations that also include articles on their design and use are provided by Zuckerman and Horn (1973) and Stadsklev (1974–1975). *Serious Games* (Abt, 1970) and *Simulation Games: An Approach to Learning* (Adams, 1973) provide general discussions of this teaching/learning strategy. Greenblat and Duke (1975) have edited a very informative collection of articles, *Gaming-Simulation: Rationale, Design, and Applications.*

Total Immersion

Outward Bound, Inc., serves more than 5000 students each year. They publish an annual listing of courses, available from 165 West Putnam Avenue, Greenwich, Connecticut 06830.

After seeing the movie *Walkabout,* the story of an Australian aborigine on a six-month solo, one educator began speculating: What could be an appropriate walkabout for American high school graduates? Some people might want a wilderness experience, others would display technological expertise, and still others might be most concerned about their sensitivities to people or their creative artistic expression or their facility with abstract ideas. His article could be used to design personal walkabout experiences (Gibbons, 1974).

Learners as Teachers

Having students learn from other students is one means of fostering cooperation. An interesting discussion of the benefit of cooperative learning activities is "Instructional Goal Structure: Cooperative, Competitive, or Individualistic" (Johnson & Johnson, 1974). The authors describe the advantages and disadvantages of each of those three goal structures and suggest instructional procedures compatible with each.

Additional illustrations of learning together among equals are given in "Self-directed Student Groups and College Learning" (Beach, 1974) and in "Peer Teaching: A Description and Evaluation" (McNall, 1975).

Numerous illustrations of tutoring projects and a statement of rationale for their use is given in *Children Teach Children: Learning by Teaching* (Gartner, Kohler, & Riessman, 1971). In *Tutoring with Students,* Melaragno (1976) offers step-by-step instructions for establishing tutoring programs.

Learning Exchanges

The Learning Exchange in Evanston may be reached at P.O. Box 920, Evanston, Illinois 60204. In other parts of the country learning networks may have telephone listings or may advertise in community-oriented newspapers or on radio stations. Local growth centers or campus student unions would probably know about nearby exchanges or may even have started their own. The Learning Exchange in Evanston will supply a list of other networks on request.

CHAPTER
FOUR

THE TEACHER
AS HELPER

Most teaching/learning activities emphasize the "thinking" capacity of learners. Their emotional life is likely to be deemphasized in formal education to the extent that attention is lavished on their cognitive development. Learners are expected to feel good about learning and about what is learned, to be sure, but the processes of feeling—the way emotions are learned, the way feelings are expressed—are considered irrelevant, or even distracting, to the business of teaching and learning. The teacher as helper attempts to correct this imbalance and places emphasis on how feelings and emotions are learned and expressed.

Feelings can hardly be barred from school. Both learner and teacher bring feelings on a multitude of topics to school, and those feelings are easily triggered by the learning process. Attention to feelings is most often limited to superficial attempts to help everyone "get along with others." Consequently, genuine feelings, especially negative ones, are more often suppressed than expressed; they are made to seem an illegitimate rather than a valuable part of the self. Since so many people spend so much of their time with other persons, repressive "getting along" is hardly a fulfilling model for adult life. As a result, young people are forced to learn how to relate to others through haphazard trial and error in settings other than education.

Another reason that schools do not much concern themselves with emotional development is the difficulty of articulating feelings. Paradoxically, the institution where people should learn to communicate with others is preoccupied with those symbols that are most easily dealt with; it avoids communication that is difficult.

What are these difficult things? By and large they are the feelings: the things that are hard to explain because they are not well-formed concepts. They cannot be written on blackboards, for the words haven't yet taken sufficient form that we can write them. They are not just the feelings, though; they are also half-formed ideas. Sometimes they are barely conscious things. Always they are potentially creative. Were

61

they to be heard, they would supply everybody with new information. One way of defining a school is to say that it is a place which puts a high premium on saying things well. Students and teachers value looking good to one another and among themselves. Look good! Say smart things! Approval and evaluation, of teachers and of students, is very important in school. What the whole evaluation system is about is appearance: "Above all, look good!" [Coulson, 1972, pp. 25–26].

Emphasis on "looking good" discourages taking risks; so, as Coulson says, people take their feelings "into hiding." Affective life is inhibited. Interpersonal relations are not genuine. Until some competence can be gained in the interpersonal communication of feeling, learners are unlikely to feel fulfilled or to be able to identify why they are unfulfilled. Two charges are implicit in Coulson's remarks. One deals with feelings and the other with tentatively held ideas. He contends that classrooms fail to elicit either of these kinds of communications. Indeed, feelings and tentative expressions are actually suppressed if classrooms elicit only that which is easily articulated.

Evidence to support these charges is available. First, concerning tentative ideas or hunches, a study by Goodlad is representative. His research team observed 150 elementary classrooms in 67 schools in 26 districts across the country.

Even at kindergarten and first-grade levels, most of the instruction emphasized the ability to remember, to recognize from previous exposure, and to repeat. The symbol for mastery was the accuracy of verbal responses—usually, as stated before, responses to teacher questions. When higher intellectual processes were sought or elicited, they usually involved some display of reading or mathematical comprehension. There was little exploring, hunching, guessing, supposing, at any grade level. The teacher-to-child pattern of interaction apparently was not conducive to this sort of inquiry [Goodlad et al., 1970, p. 53].

Research on verbal behavior in classrooms shows overwhelming teacher domination and preoccupation with content. Flanders has formulated what he calls "the rule of two-thirds": two-thirds of the time someone is talking in a typical classroom; two-thirds of that talk is done by the teacher; and two-thirds of that teacher-talk is directive (that is, lecturing, giving directions, or criticizing). During some of the remaining time the teacher may use indirect influence, which includes attention to feelings, but that is a very small proportion of time. Teacher domination is even greater in classes of low-achieving students (but not so great in classes of high-achieving students) (Flanders, 1963). In a study of first-, sixth-, and eleventh-grade classrooms, Adams and Biddle (1970) found that 84% of communication episodes were teacher dominated and that less than .5% dealt with feelings or interpersonal relations. That is, only 1 out of 200 incidents of verbal behavior was concerned with either the relations between pupils or their feelings.

There is some evidence that superior elementary teachers respond to feelings more frequently than average teachers, about three times as often, although the average incidence is still relatively low (Amidon & Giammatteo, 1967).

Most of this research has dealt with elementary teachers. It is probably worth noting that the findings represent averages across a number of teachers. Rather than identifying "direct teachers" and "indirect teachers," since any teacher is more or less directive from time to time, the research documents the *relative* incidence of teacher behavior. In so doing, it paints a representative picture of typical pupil experiences accumulated across years of schooling.

In high schools and colleges one might expect more tolerance of guesses, hypotheses, and hunches related to subject matter, but I can find no research evidence for greater expression and acceptance of feelings. It may be that emotion-laden discussions do occur outside of classrooms. Expression of feelings may be considered legitimate as a kind of counseling function of the teacher. While that is to be encouraged, it is not a sufficient expression of the teacher's helping role.

This chapter examines two communication patterns in which feelings are attended to as part of the learning process. One pattern focuses on the teacher's communication with individual students (alone and in a group) and includes some of the skills underlying empathic communication. The second communication pattern focuses on peer support in groups. Here the group itself is the teacher. Members help themselves and each other rather than primarily being helped by an expert. This pattern is illustrated by encounter and T-groups and by such self-help groups as Alcoholics Anonymous.

Two broad assumptions underlie the teacher's role as helper. One is that understanding and expressing feelings is instrumental for subject-matter learning; that is, a healthy emotional climate in the learning environment facilitates learning. Second, the teacher as helper considers facility in communicating feelings to be important in itself. People are more mature when they are sensitive to the feelings of others and to their own, and when they are skilled at sending and receiving feeling-laden messages. According to this assumption, educational programs should deal with feelings and emotions as *parts of their content* as well as means for facilitating subject-matter learning.

THE TEACHER AS HELPER: EMPATHIC COMMUNICATION

This section discusses the teacher's role in communicating with individuals or with classroom groups. The next section discusses the group as a whole, including the teacher, as it facilitates and supports the articulation and understanding of feelings.

EMPATHIC RESPONSES

Suppose you are a teacher. (If you cannot picture yourself as a teacher, imagine that a good friend has sought you out.) A student, looking depressed, comes to you saying "I feel really bad. My grades are going to be so lousy this time." How do you respond? Take a moment to write down the first words you would say in response to that person's statement.

Now consider some of the possible responses. Naturally, they will vary according to the speaker's style of communication and appraisal of the situation. Here are some likely responses.

> Learner: "I feel really bad. My grades are going to be so lousy this time."
> Teacher 1: "What do you think your grades will be?"
> Teacher 2: "With your average? It can't hurt you much."
> Teacher 3: "That's because you always ask too much of yourself."
> Teacher 4: "Everybody has some good times and some bad times."
> Teacher 5: "If your grades look bad, everything else must look pretty bad too."

Now check your own feelings. How would you feel if a teacher made these comments to you?

Each of these responses implies something about how the other person's needs are interpreted. The first *probes* for more information, probably hoping to make the situation seem more positive. Perhaps things won't look so bad after all. The response does not, however, deal with the feelings directly. The second response *evaluates*. It sounds a bit argumentative and may cut off further exploration. Instead of acknowledging the feelings, this response denies the legitimacy of the feelings. With your average, it says, you have no right to feel bad. The third *interprets*. It offers a reason for the feelings. The reason may satisfy the interpreter, but it is likely to strike the student as premature, threatening, wrong, or just plain boring. The fourth *reassures*. It may show sympathy ("I know how it feels"), but it may also belittle the feelings and seem patronizing. The last response shows *empathy*. It attempts to acknowledge and accept the feelings and to restate them in a clarifying way. (These categories are based on Erb & Hooker, 1967.)

Now go back and decide which category best describes the response you would have made.

Certainly each response can be helpful and appropriate in one situation or another. Nevertheless, if you wish to assist someone to explore a problem, empathic responding is most effective. In the helping role, great care must be taken to be open, to avoid premature closing of a conversation. Evaluating, interpreting, or reassuring responses are likely to cut off further dialog. Probing continues the conversation but usually fails to acknowledge the depth of feeling. Ideally, an empathic response catches the feeling and reflects it back to the speaker with a bit of awareness that is new to the speaker. In this example, the learner may not have been aware how much feelings about grades color feelings about other things. The response includes that awareness: "If your grades look bad, everything else must look pretty bad too." When effective, the empathic response legitimizes subsequent communication of feelings as well as of information. At the personal level, the empathic response makes the recipient feel as if he or she is "seeing myself through my own eyes."

There is general agreement about the desirability of empathy in communication. Carl Rogers (1951) and Robert Carkhuff (1969) in particular discuss these issues and describe training procedures for increasing empathy. Yet most people experience difficulty in displaying greater empathy. I believe this is because empathy requires close identification with another person, and most of us are used to seeing others primarily in terms of ourselves. We evaluate or interpret or reassure in ways that suggest we have an answer: "I know exactly how you feel. Why, just the other day, I . . . . " Such a statement *declares* empathy ("I know exactly how you feel") but fails to *demonstrate* empathy. Instead, the statement seems to impose one person's solution on another person. Empathy requires a denial of self in order to respond as if one were the other person.

Such a denial of self in order to reach another person may be easier for those who are in touch with their own feelings. In the following section we examine a way of more accurately expressing one's own feelings to others.

I-MESSAGES

Sending feelings to another is as important for effective communication as accurately receiving feelings from the other. Classroom observation suggests that teachers are more likely to send blame in a message than to describe their feelings in a revealing way. For example, if a child is habitually late with work, the teacher naturally feels anger. The most frequent response is a blaming response: "You never do your assignment!" The teacher thereby judges the student and sends a you-message, a message in which the learner may hear "You never do your assignment, and what an awful kid you are!"

The teacher probably did not wish to be so harsh, if only because that approach will hurt the relationship in the future. Suppose the teacher had said "I feel really defeated when you don't do your assignments and I have to give you a low grade." In that statement the teacher has been fairly specific, so that the student might infer "What I need to do to make my work better is just to get the stuff done on time." This is an I-message: the teacher gives a revealing *self*-description and takes responsibility for feelings rather than distorting the feelings into some bad quality of the learner.

I-messages are an important skill in Teacher Effectiveness Training Workshops originated by Thomas Gordon, a former colleague of Carl Rogers. Gordon (1974) describes three components of an effective I-message. First, the I-message describes what is causing the problem for the teacher—for example, "When you don't do your assignment." This should be a statement of fact as free from judgment as possible. Second, an I-message states the consequence of the student's behavior for the teacher: "and I have to give you a low grade." This consequence would be news to any student who believes that teachers love to give low grades. Finally, the I-message states the teacher's feelings: "I feel really defeated." This too may be news to students who believe that teachers don't care. The description should be as precise and accurate as possible; for example, "defeated" is more precise than "upset."

I-messages may be positive as well as negative. A learner should enjoy hearing "I really feel proud of you when you put all the materials back on the shelves and I don't have to stay late to do it."

TWO CLASSROOM DISCUSSIONS

A teacher adopting the helper's role must be skilled in expressing empathy, in sending I-messages, and in identifying possible solutions to conflicts. These skills are illustrated in the following classroom discussions (contributed by two Teacher Effectiveness Training instructors, Roland Larson and Dorothy Williams).

1. The teacher and students are experiencing a conflict over a class assignment. As they engage in mutual problem solving, the teacher

shows respect for and trust in the students and expresses his own needs clearly.

>TEACHER: Two weeks from today, at the end of our unit on Europe, I want each of you to hand in three maps of Europe, colored by individual country, to show the national boundaries as they were in 1914, 1918, and . . .
>
>STUDENT: (groaning) Oh, not another of those map things.
>
>TEACHER: You're pretty tired of drawing maps. (empathy)
>
>SEVERAL STUDENTS: Boy, are we ever. . . . I thought I was all through coloring stuff in the third grade. . . . Anything but maps. . . .
>
>TEACHER: Well, that presents a problem, doesn't it? I think it is important with this unit for you to do something that involves some use of references or sources other than the geography textbook, and something that involves some kind of activity other than reading and discussing, which is what we do most of the time. I know some of you like the map drawing we've done before, but I guess you don't all like doing maps that much. (problem solving)
>
>SEVERAL STUDENTS: (with vigorous nods) Right.
>
>TEACHER: Well, has anybody got any ideas?
>
>STUDENT: How about having us do things that can be presented to the class? Then we can learn something from what other kids did. (some assent, some groans)
>
>TEACHER: Some of you like that, but some of you aren't too wild about presenting reports to the class. (empathy)
>
>SAME STUDENT: Well, it could be stuff to show. It wouldn't have to be all reports and getting up and talking to the class.
>
>TEACHER: Something *like* maps, but not necessarily maps, that would *show* something that might be helpful to other students. You wouldn't have to talk. How does that sound? (problem solving) (general assent)
>
>TEACHER: I still have a problem with there being too many different kinds of projects going on, because, let's face it, I may have to spend time checking information on 15 or 20 projects if you all do different ones. I don't have time for that. I guess I'd feel better if we tried, say, four different kinds of projects. Could we limit it to 4? (I-message) (general agreement)
>
>STUDENT: That's OK if they're interesting. What did you have in mind?
>
>TEACHER: (to total class) I'd like to know what you have in mind.
>
>STUDENT: Before we went to Europe, I saw a slide show that a family did about *their* trip to Europe. They had music on tape to go with it, and a script, and everything. I have some slides from our trip, and I could work with some other kids who wanted to work on music and a script and arranging the slides, and stuff. (some enthusiasm, with five persons volunteering to work with him)

TEACHER: So there are six working on a slide presentation. Any-
body else have an idea for a group project? Or for something you
could do independently that others might also like to do independently?

The outcome of the discussion was that several students stuck with
the map project. Three Jewish students, working independently, taped
interviews with their parents or with friends who had been interned in
German concentration camps during World War II. Several math students
worked out tables on per capita income in several European countries at
five-year intervals and discussed them with the class.

The willingness of that teacher to deal with his own feelings and
with the feelings of his students brought about a solution to the conflict
over the assignment that facilitated much richer learning. The unit on
Europe was a better experience than originally planned.

2. The following example involves conflict over rule setting.
Can you find instances of empathy, I-messages, and problem solving?
In this situation the principal has mentioned to a particular sixth-grade
teacher that he has the impression children are leaving the teacher's room
too freely. He is afraid that this amount of coming and going may be
disturbing to other classes.

TEACHER: Up to now, this year, you've been leaving the room
whenever you want to, without asking, and I've been trusting you
to come back when you have finished your errand. But lately
too many people are gone at once, or are staying too long. I think
I may get in trouble with the principal and with some of the other
teachers if we don't figure out some way we can take care of this
problem.
CHILD: How about if we just ask you when we want to leave and
you tell us whether we can or not?
TEACHER: That would bother me, because often I'm busy working
with a group of five or ten people, and I don't want to have to
stop what we are doing every three or four minutes to have you
check with me about leaving.
CHILD: Well, how about making a rule that nobody leaves?
SEVERAL CHILDREN: Oh, no! We have to be able to leave. . . . I
have to go to the library to get stuff for my report. . . . I leave
for my clarinet lesson once a week.
TEACHER: It seems pretty necessary for some of you to be gone
some of the time, but we have to figure out how to do it so we
don't bother other people. Sometimes, too, like when we're taking
a test, or getting ready for a total class project, everybody needs
to be here at once. Any ideas?
CHILD: How about if we keep a list up by the door, and we sign
our name and where we're going, and then cross it off when we
get back?

CHILD: Or one person could just keep track who goes out and where, and like that? I wouldn't want to do it all the time, but sometimes it would be OK.

CHILD: Well, we could take turns doing that.

TEACHER: You would be willing as a class to take turns with the responsibility of knowing where people are, being a kind of traffic manager?

SEVERAL CHILDREN: Yeah. . . . I'll do it first. . . . I'll do it.

TEACHER: You like that way of doing it better than having a list posted by the door? (nods and assents)

CHILD: Yeah, but what if the person being traffic manager is mad at you and won't let you go?

CHILD: And how does that keep a lot of us from being gone at once?

CHILD: Let's say no more than three of us can be gone at once, and the traffic manager has to know where everybody is, and he has to let you be gone if you want to.

TEACHER: You like the idea of a number limit? (general agreement) I guess I like that, too. Then that doesn't leave us a chance to argue about how many is too many.

CHILD: (confirming) So then the kid who does it can't keep you from leaving if there aren't three gone.

OTHER CHILDREN: Right.

TEACHER: That all sounds good to me. Should we try it this week and see how it works out? Oh, and how about times when I need to have you all here?

CHILD: Well, you could just tell us, like, at 10 we're going to do something, so from 10 to 10:30 nobody should plan to leave, and then we wouldn't. How's that?

TEACHER: Is that solution OK with everybody? It's OK with me. Now let's be sure we understand it all. The traffic manager will keep a written list of who goes out and where. Shall we have that person serve for a week at a time? OK with everybody? (nods around room) Any person may leave at any time, after first checking with the traffic manager, as long as there are no more than two people gone already. And I'll let you know ahead of time when we will need to have everyone here. OK? OK.

This teacher has been successful in *helping* students rather than merely setting and imposing rules.

Sending I-messages and responding with empathy are not easy. For example, many of us do not have a sufficient vocabulary of words that describe personal feelings that we sense in others. In that case vocabulary exercises may be appropriate. Wittmer and Myrick (1974) provide lists of feeling terms, both positive and negative, and of empathic-sounding sentences that may be helpful for practice. Using such exercises and practicing with friends should be useful for improving these communications skills.

THE GROUP AS HELPER

Opportunities to experience warmth and intimacy seem to be declining in our society. These experiences have been part of traditional family life, but families are less stable than in the past. There is more divorce, remarriage, and unmarried cohabitation. Compared with family patterns in the past, each of these reduces the stability and duration of family relationships. Religious institutions have apparently been unable to change this trend, and schools, as we have seen, minimize the understanding and expression of feelings as they emphasize competitive subject-matter learning.

I believe these developments are largely responsible for the emergence of "the group phenomenon." This phenomenon has established small groups of strangers, temporary societies, as places where individuals can receive emotional support and can experience intimacy and warmth. These are groups for the healthy and for the mildly troubled. They are for persons functioning *despite* their problems and for those who function well but feel a need to grow further in interpersonal relationships. These groups exist not because members are certifiably sick (as in therapy groups), not because of a common task or interest (election campaigning, great books), and not simply for social contact. They exist as manifestations of a realization that everyone needs to belong and to learn from others in a group. Since older institutions of society do not meet these needs as they once did, new group forms have emerged.

Groups serve the needs of individuals through processes that are distinctive to the group setting.

> The newcomer finds himself listened to, responded to; he discovers that he makes sense, can articulate feelings and reach out to others, be accepted, understood, appreciated, responded to closely. He discovers that there is room for him as a person and not just as a maker of canned, appropriate statements or as a player of prescribed roles. His previously almost dumb and silent self becomes intensely alive, being in this group is intense and it is growth-producing. He "breaks through," finds himself as not just a player of roles, but also as speaking from himself as an experiencing, feeling, human being [Gendlin, 1970, p. 557].

The group provides an opportunity to learn interpersonal skills that were not learned earlier and to enhance skills that were incompletely learned.

To emphasize the differences between this setting for learning and those settings we have previously considered, I shall summarize three characteristics of learning in interpersonal settings (based on Menges & McGaghie, 1974).

1. First, the *setting* is distinctive in that it depends on the presence of others. People volunteer for participation. They are present out of decision, not out of coercion. If the group serves no useful purpose for them, they need attend no longer. Members are thus self-selected, and the group exists only because it is somehow at their service. In cognitive learning, the learner customarily deals with nonresponsive entities—for example, bits of information. In contrast, interpersonal learning requires that the learner deal not with nonresponsive objects but with responsive subjects—that is, people. Interpersonal learning can occur only in an interpersonal setting.

2. The *method* is experiential. The group member learns with more directness and immediacy than in cognitive learning. One does not seek "knowledge about" something. Nor does one vicariously assimilate accounts of personal experiences. Instead, one gains direct personal knowledge of others by shared experiencing. "Synnoetics" is the term Phenix uses to describe meanings "in which a person has a direct insight into other beings (or oneself) as concrete wholes existing in relation" (1964, p. 193). He points out that such learning differs from the manipulation of symbols (cognitive learning) in several ways. Personal knowledge requires engagement rather than detachment. It involves intersubjectivity (the relation of subject to subject) rather than objectivity (the relation of subject to object); "the separation between subject and object is overcome and a personal meeting takes place" (Phenix, 1964, p. 194). It involves meanings that are concrete rather than meanings that are abstractions from some other, more complete experience. Finally, it is existential: personal knowledge has to do with *being itself* rather than with kinds and qualities of being. Reading this chapter may provide *knowledge about* how groups facilitate learning, but only *participation* in groups can produce personal knowledge and interpersonal learning.

3. The desired *outcomes* are more varied than those of subject-matter learning. Members and leaders are likely to make rather general statements of objectives and expectations. "I want to be more confident and more outgoing." "I want to be more in touch with my feelings." "I want to get closer to people." "I want to have more self-control." If members later say that they have come to feel more positive about themselves, can the group be considered a success? Should such changes in self-concept be accompanied by changes noted by friends or fellow workers, by higher grades, by better job performance? Research on these questions is discussed later in the chapter.

The next sections examine two types of group experience that differ in both process and outcome: first, encounter and training groups, and, second, self-help groups.

All these groups are, of course, much more temporary than the families that most persons have experienced. But unlike some family and social experiences, these groups are powerful vehicles for self-examination in a supportive environment, for learning ways of relating to others, and especially for learning how to express the feelings involved in relationships.

ENCOUNTER GROUPS: FACILITATING PERSONAL GROWTH

What is encounter? In 1912 Jacob Moreno used the metaphor of two persons exchanging eyes in order to know each other better. "A meeting of two: eye to eye, face to face. And when you are near I will tear your eyes out and place them instead of mine, and you will tear my eyes out and will place them instead of yours, then I will look at you with your eyes and you will look at me with mine" (quoted in Ruitenbeek, 1970, p. 17). Encounter-group meetings are social occasions where one may come to see the world as others perceive it and see oneself as perceived by others. These perceptions do not come without pain, but they bring rewards and deep satisfactions.

Imagine what it is like to participate in such a group. Let us assume that the group is scheduled over a weekend. Some participants arrive at the scheduled college dorm in time for dinner Friday and learn that ten others are expected. Those already present vary in age, race, sex, occupation, and other characteristics. There is a leader, called a facilitator in the brochure. The announced schedule is 8–11 P.M. on Friday, 9 A.M.– 9 P.M. on Saturday, and 10 A.M.–2 P.M. on Sunday. Meals will be eaten together in the dorm, and most participants will sleep there.

The group gathers in the lounge, and the leader makes some general introductory remarks. He explains that this group belongs to all members to do with as they please. There is no set agenda, and the only goal is that each member come to know the other members better. He encourages participants to *be* in the group as totally as possible, to experiment with new ways of relating to people, to try some risky things. He seems tentative, almost uncertain, in his expectations. "We really can make of it anything we want to make of it, and, for myself, I don't have any prediction, except that by the time we end Sunday afternoon, we'll probably know each other a lot better than we do right now; but how we may want to go about it, or what we want to do, that's really up to us" (Carl Rogers, quoted in Coulson, 1970, p. 1).

What happens after that rather ambiguous start? There is no list of problems to be solved, no agenda of tasks to be attacked. There is nothing to do except what the members wish to do. And that, of course, is different for every group. Usually, social chitchat consumes some time and is followed by expressions of dissatisfaction by members who hope that *something* more significant will happen. Then comes a realization that if the leader won't make things happen, the members must. So people begin to speak more freely about how they feel, about things they feel good about and things that bother them, often referring to events that have happened in the group. In one group a member described his impression of Sam, commenting on his inner strength. Sam replied:

> Perhaps I'm not aware of or experiencing it that way, as strength. (Pause.) I think, when I was talking with, I think it was the first day I was talking to you, Tom, when in the course of that, I expressed a *genuine surprise* I had, the first time I realized that I could *frighten* someone—It really, it was a discovery that I had to just kind of look at and feel and get to know, you know, it was such a *new* experience for me. I was so used to the feeling of being frightened by *others* that it had never occurred to me that anyone could be—I guess it *never had*—that anyone could be frightened of *me*. And I guess maybe it has something to do with how I feel about myself [Rogers, 1970, p. 20].*

Sam is learning how others perceive him and is modifying his self-perception as a result.

In the openness of a group, a person can reveal personal aspects in ways that are stifled in ordinary social situations. Group members begin to show trust and acceptance for one another. One woman who was very unhappy with herself and whose marriage was on the rocks joined a group almost as a last resort. In writing later to another participant she says:

> . . . the real turning point for me was a simple gesture on your part of putting your arm around my shoulder one afternoon when I had made some crack about you not being a member of the group—that no one could cry on your shoulder. In my notes I had written the night before, "There is no man in the world who loves me!" You seemed so genuinely concerned that day that I was overwhelmed. . . . I received the gesture as one of the first feelings of acceptance—of me, just the dumb way I am, prickles and all—that I had ever experienced. I have felt needed, loving, competent, furious, frantic, anything and everything but just plain *loved*. You can imagine the flood of gratitude, humility, release that swept over me. I wrote with considerable joy, "*I* actually felt *loved*" [quoted in Rogers, 1970, p. 34].

*From *Carl Rogers on Encounter Groups,* by C. Rogers. Copyright 1970 by Harper & Row Publishers. This and all other quotations from this source are reprinted by permission.

As the group proceeds, a certain pattern of development is likely. There is greater investment of emotion by members, more willingness to share with others, and more concern to react honestly to others. Figure 4-1 provides a hypothetical sampling of members' responses at three points during a group's history. There is a beginning in uncertainty, hesitation, and apprehension. Then there is progress through tentative participation to emotional commitment, risk taking, and feelings of security (Lakin, 1972).

Experiencing these changes is powerful, and they usually produce very positive evaluations of the group experience. Many members experience a "psychological high" for weeks, feeling themselves more in touch with their strengths and capacities. One educator wrote how wonderful it felt when she went to school on the Monday after her weekend group as Margaret the person, instead of Margaret the principal.

Openness, awareness, and intimacy of communication are valued and celebrated in encounter and sensitivity-training groups. The group is a contrived social event that counteracts the emptiness felt in much interpersonal contact. It is an occasion that gives people permission to be different than they ordinarily are. Further, it helps people learn their own power to *create* such occasions. Near the end of one group, a member expressed with deep feeling what he had learned: "People can be concerned but I never would have thought somone could be concerned over *me,* no matter if we sat here for a month" (Coulson, 1970, p. 5), and later, "I learned that this could happen not just here but any place I want it to happen" (Coulson, 1970, p. 24). Thus one comes to see considerably more freedom in life than was apparent previously. This man now knows that he can make groups happen. "The foremost learning of an encounter group is a procedural learning: one learns he can call on people. No small learning" (Coulson, 1970, p. 24).

Not all reaction to encounter groups has been enthusiastic. The potential for intense emotional expression is a potential for destructiveness as well as for positive learning. The movement has attracted "gurus," some of whom are regarded with undisguised hostility by established psychologists. Their "tools" include massage, nudity, group fantasy, marathons, and monitoring of brain waves. Some critics predict that uncontrolled sexual and aggressive behavior is fostered in such groups. Others fear that serious psychological disorders will be precipitated and are concerned about the proper training of group leaders. "Many people in our contemporary society are sitting on explosive bombs, but for some reason or another they are never exploded. However the group experience, such as an encounter group, might just do the trick and who is there to recognize this and moreover to help and understand?" (Ruitenbeek, 1970, p. 169).

Figure 4-1. Reactions of a group member at three points in a group's life

Reactions Early in the Group	Reactions Midway in the Group	Reactions Late in the Group
1. I'll wait and see what happens.	1. We're going around in circles. What can I do to help?	1. I seem to care a lot about this group.
2. It feels very tense in here.	2. Some of these people are OK when you see them outside the group.	2. I got emotional when Mike talked about what he learned from us.
3. I'd like to ask the leader what he's up to, but I'd better not.	3. I'll try starting today. Let's see what happens.	3. I wish Sue could share with us. What's blocking her in the group?
4. What am I supposed to do?	4. Got to "level" (be more direct).	4. Bob always changes the subject just when we're getting someplace. I'll tell him how it makes me feel.
5. I feel "out of it."	5. If I speak out, Carl will clobber me.	5. Why won't Sal stick his neck out?
6. Whom can I trust?	6. Maybe Hal will understand and come through for me.	6. OK, I'll try telling you how you just now made me feel.
7. I want to get something started, but how?	7. What do I care whether they like me or not?	7. Look, don't fence me in. We can't agree about everything.
8. This conversation is irrelevant.	8. What have I said that hurt Irving?	8. What went on really concerned each of us.
9. Nobody seems to care about what I say.	9. How do we make Jean feel a part of the group?	9. I never thought Tanya would reach out the way she did to Harry.
10. I think other groups have got to be better than this one.	10. I see other groups have their troubles, too. We're not the only ones.	10. I've only just begun to understand some important things!

Adapted from *Experiential Groups: The Uses of Interpersonal Encounter, Psychotherapy Groups, and Sensitivity Training*, by M. Lakin. Copyright 1972 by Silver Burdett Company. Reprinted by permission.

Other critics, usually nonpsychologists who write rather shrilly, find groups a threat to the American way of life rather than a force for positive change. An article in *Law and Order* magazine, for example, equates sensitivity training with brainwashing and accuses it of fostering group dependency, sacrificing individualism, and altering or destroying attitudes. "At the base of this sensitivity training technique lies an ideological war against the entire warp and woof of the American culture. It deserves to be recognized for what it is" (quoted in Golembiewski & Blumberg, 1970, p. 256).

The press has given relatively more attention to groups than has the scientific community. Many accounts have appeared in national magazines. There are fictionalized treatments, too, such as *The Lemon Eaters,* a serious novel by Jerry Sohl (1968). Unfortunately its jacket copy is illustrated with a female nude and calls it "a novel about a nonstop weekend of emotional striptease." Two novels have been written by group leaders on the group experience: *Encounter* (Mann, 1971) and *Marathon 16* (Shepard & Lee, 1971). Do-it-yourself guides have appeared; for example, *Conduct Your Own Awareness Sessions,* "the amazing sensitivity techniques that are making happiness a reality for thousands" (Hills & Stone, 1970). This attention indicates the wide public interest in encounter. Unfortunately, much of that interest is inspired by the faddish fringes of the movement.

Schools have been reluctant to identify with these activities. It is true that teachers are not likely to become leaders of classroom encounter groups for their students; nonetheless the group experience may be very beneficial for teachers who are seeking personal growth. In selecting a group for personal growth, several cautions are necessary. First, be sure it is affiliated with an established agency. Responsible groups are often run through mental health centers, YMCA's, college counseling agencies, and growth centers. Second, determine what previous experience and/or training in group work the leader has had. Third, secure a description of the group's goals and activities. Any leader unwilling or unable to describe goals and activities in some detail is probably not worthy of the trust members must give if the group is to be successful. Prospective members cannot choose among available groups without such information.

TRAINING GROUPS: FACILITATING PROFESSIONAL GROWTH

The encounter-group movement has developed around attempts to enhance *personal* growth. Another focus for groups involves persons in their job or community settings and seeks to enhance *professional* growth. Groups have been developed to improve human relations in areas of racial tension and to improve communication skills so that an organization runs more smoothly. Teacher Effectiveness Training (Gordon, 1974) was referred to earlier in this chapter and exemplifies the use of a group setting to deal with particular skills, for example sending I-messages, so that a person becomes more effective as a professional.

Training groups, or T-groups, have somewhat more specific goals than encounter groups have. They attempt to foster professional as well as personal growth and generally use somewhat more structured activities than do personal-growth groups. The major credit for developing laboratory programs in interpersonal behavior with applications to social and organizational change goes to the National Training Laboratories. Since 1947, NTL has offered summer workshops for professionals, often advertised for particular groups—middle managers, negotiators, graduate students, Black professionals, and so on. Consequently there is some homogeneity among the job settings of participants in a particular group.

The Basic Human Interaction Laboratory is probably the least structured of the NTL programs and likely to attract the most heterogeneous clientele. But it too includes a number of structured activities.

> At the core of this two-week residential program is a small group experience, the T-Group. During this time, participants create a group in which members can learn from one another, compare the consequences of their behavior with their intentions, see the range of different perceptions of any given act, determine if they might wish to change, and—if they do—experiment with new ways of behavior. In addition to the T-Group, the lab includes opportunities for other small group mixtures, large group (community) sessions, theory sessions, interpersonal skill-building and practice sessions, intergroup exercises, role playing and other "experience-based" activities [National Training Laboratories Institute, 1975].

Since group members spend considerable time working on common tasks supplied by the trainer, members do not simply react to one another's personal responses to having nothing to do (the characteristic situation of an agendaless encounter group). Instead, they receive feedback on behavior in a setting that to some extent resembles the work setting back home. Applying lab experiences to daily life outside the lab is continually encouraged by the staff. There is also cognitive input. Findings from social-science research and other information may be supplied in written or lecture form.

Two other training-group approaches are described below. One deals primarily with members of business organizations. The other is aimed at students as well as at persons in business.

Grid Seminars for organizational development. One of the largest consulting firms specializing in organizational development is Scientific Methods, Inc., of Austin, Texas. Robert Blake, a former professor of psychology, heads this firm with branches around the world. The training he offers is highly directive and structured. "In our view," he says, "it's a very wasteful thing for people to flounder around in labs trying to decide *what* to learn, when they're there to learn something, and designs for them to learn it do exist" (quoted in Howard, 1970, p. 47).

Blake's design is called the Managerial Grid. It is a nine-category grid representing the managerial styles of individuals. One axis represents concerns with people and the other represents concerns with production. A participant's style is identified through questionnaires and plotted in one of the 81 cells of the grid. Successful training moves each person toward the ideal position. At that position both concern for people and concern for production are maximized: "Work accomplishment is from committed people; interdependence through a 'common stake' in organization purpose leads to relationships of trust and respect" (Blake et al., 1970, p. 393).

The grid is the reference point throughout an extensive six-phase educational program that may extend from three to six years. The educational steps include:

> An investigation by each man of his own managerial style, using certain Managerial Grid forms of analysis. These include self-evaluation instruments, self-administered learning quizzes, in-basket procedures, and organizational simulations.
> A detailed and repeated evaluation of team effectiveness by groups which work with each other.
> Diagnosis of major organization problem areas; e.g., long-range planning, profitability of operation, union-management relations, promotion policies, incentive awards, new-product development, absenteeism, utilities conservation, and safety [Blake et al., 1970, p. 392].

Many training devices are in the form of problems to be solved by teams. The emphasis is on reducing conflict by learning to substitute joint problem solving for a conflictful win-lose pattern. Progress can be evaluated at any point by once again plotting positions on the grid. The grid provides individual feedback; additional feedback comes from personal communication with other participants. Careful distinctions are made, however, between comments relating to personal behavior and comments relating to managerial style, and the former are not encouraged.

Blake has reported data on the success of the Managerial Grid for a variety of businesses. Its use seems to be related to production-cost savings and increases in productivity as well as improved boss-subordinate, group and intergroup relations among managers (Blake et al., 1970).

Increasing achievement motivation. Psychologists have long speculated that if people could be made to think more highly of themselves and their abilities they would achieve more. Some have attempted to test this assumption, using a variety of training procedures and assessing effects on various kinds of achievement.

Persons who are highly motivated to achieve have been found to display characteristic thought patterns and action strategies. They place primary emphasis on attaining excellence rather than on fostering particular kinds of relationships with other people. They think carefully about what success or failure would be like. When they take action, they prefer situations in which they can take calculated, realistic risks, take personal responsibility, and receive immediate, concrete feedback about their performance. They have a great deal of initiative, confidence, and feeling for innovation. They work hard, not just for reward, but because they take pride in good work (Alschuler, 1968).

Many achievement-motivation training programs have been highly successful. Increases in business diversification, promotion rates, and grades have been reported (Alschuler, 1973). Courses on achievement motivation typically use exercises based on the identification of strengths and successes. Participants may be asked to list successes they experienced during a particular time in their lives and to indicate why they consider them successes. They may also be asked to identify the reward or payoff that was important for each success.

A particular training program emphasizes the following goals:

1. The first goal is to develop a constructive dialogue with one's own fantasy life. Achievement-motivation students are taught to imagine doing things very well, to distinguish between achievement imagery and task imagery, and to carefully plan projects that will make it possible for them to reach the images they seek. Not only does this process often help students become aware of previously ignored aspects of their own personality, it is often a joyful and enhancing experience as well.

2. The second goal involves the development of nonverbal understanding and communication skills. Examples of techniques used to achieve this goal include silent-theater improvisations, meditation, and a wide variety of games such as target games for teaching moderate risk taking. In such a game students learn to make realistic estimates of their performance by receiving the maximum number of points for exactly making the "bid." Fewer points are earned for overestimates or underestimates. These games are designed for stimulating the kind of learning that can be carried over into real-life situations (Alschuler, 1968).

Achievement-motivation training illustrates the use of groups for enhancing professional performance in two ways. First, such training may be useful for teachers' own professional development; second, teachers may wish to provide such training for their students. After all, persons "employed" as learners have "achievement" as their professional goal. One caution is in order. For achievement-motivation training to be useful in schools, it is probably necessary that some of the constraints of traditional schooling be relaxed. For example, higher motivation to achieve is likely to be reflected in learner performance only if the school encourages learners to set their own goals and evaluate their own efforts.

RESEARCH ON ENCOUNTER AND TRAINING GROUPS

The goal of encounter groups is personal change for members. What effects have been documented? In a study of more than 1000 college students in 100 groups, Bebout characterizes results as follows:

> Members indicate greater self-satisfaction, increased self-reliance, more comfort with sexuality and less social inhibition. They feel more inner-direction, spontaneity and more acceptance of their own aggression. Self-actualizing tendencies are greater. They are less lonely and less alienated. They experience progress in a number of individual and interpersonal problems and fellow group members concur in this improvement. Members' friends report greater empathy in their relationships, and members seem less attached to shallow forms of "benevolence." Finally, in self-reports members attest to a great number of personal learnings, more self-awareness and personal growth [Bebout, 1973, p. 67].

These changes are overwhelmingly positive; not one psychiatric "casualty" was found. On the other hand, group participants did not become more productive in school or at work.

These results fairly well illustrate most research on encounter groups: positive reports about themselves from participants and from friends, few seriously harmful effects, little benefit to school or work. Lieberman, Yalom, and Miles (1973) draw more conservative conclusions from a study of more than 206 college-student participants in 17 groups. They found a higher casualty rate (although that term is a hard one to define) and found that only about one-third of the participants changed substantially in a positive direction. They reported that cognitive learning was a major characteristic of those high changers; that is, high changers reported receiving information leading to understanding and insight. This finding is important, since encounter groups are sometimes seen as avoiding cognition for exclusive immersion in feelings. Expression of feelings is probably necessary but not sufficient for achieving change in an encounter group. Cognitive analysis and reflection are apparently essential as well.

Designing scientific research on encounter is a difficult task. We have neither an adequate conceptual scheme nor appropriate research instruments to study the ineffable experience that is encounter. Skeptics find the research easy to criticize, and it is difficult to deal with their objections. Rogers says "I do feel that I could say to skeptics, if you will come with me and form a group and cut yourself off from other obligations for six or seven days so that we can meet eight to ten hours a day, you will experience something, the potency of which can't be denied. . . . This wouldn't prove anything in the scientific sense, but I don't think they could ever quite get over the fact that they had experienced a potent phenomenon that falls quite outside the tractable domain of experimental psychology" (quoted in Hart, 1970, pp. 525–526). Scientific assessment too often trivializes the experience by reducing an event to items on a questionnaire, frequency counts of supportive statements, or ratings of sensitivity by coworkers. It is not yet clear how to study the event itself rather than merely by examining variables claimed to be a part of it. Encounter is a phenomenon of undoubted power that awaits the development of appropriate tools for its comprehension.

Training groups are less affected by these research difficulties if they aim at professional rather than (or in addition to) personal growth. Since trainees at NTL and Grid Seminars are concerned with back-home organizational change, we must ask what consequences such training has for organizational functioning. First, it can be said that considerable research does show positive change. Evidence ranges from mere participant anecdotes to sophisticated and controlled studies (Campbell & Dunnette, 1968; Smith, 1975). Second, the continued patronage of training agencies suggests that clients are pleased with the results of their investment.

Yet much of this research, too, has flaws, and the rigorous researcher is likely to be critical. Consider some sources of bias common in these research designs. Effects of training are typically inferred from ratings of participants' behavior by the participant and several coworkers and are compared with ratings of others who did not receive training. But the coworkers may be influenced by their knowledge that the person they are rating has been through training; in many studies it is the participant who nominates those who will do the rating. Or participants may make only posttraining ratings of their own behavior, as in the grid study mentioned above. Comparisons are then made with how they *say* they behaved a year earlier, but such retrospective ratings are suspect. Further, the criteria on which these persons are rated have not been shown to relate to job effectiveness; that is, although the participant may hold different self-perceptions, and his or her behavior may be objectively different, the net effect on the organization may be nil or even negative.

Future research with more sensitive measures and stringent controls may document positive effects on organizations from training of individuals. For the present, however, let us assume that major organizational effects will *not* be identified and that effects will be found only for the trained individuals. Then we may speculate that the maximum effects of training would extend downward through the organizational hierarchy. That is, a person's relationships with superiors and even with colleagues would not change, but relationships with subordinates might do so. Teachers, for instance, would not transform their schools as a result of training but might make some positive changes in their classrooms.

> . . . wherever one can be in charge of his situation—as, for example, probably in his own classroom, if he is a teacher and possibly at home—then he can make positive changes; because now he knows something about what people really want, something having to do with the development of their own human potential. The group won't affect work relationships so much as what individuals do now where they *live* and in other places where their potency lies [Coulson, 1970, p. 26].

Since their institutional work setting is not where many people feel they really "live," institutions may feel no effect at all from training. However, if people feel they "live" at their work, institutional consequences may emerge.

Decisions about a social intervention with the potential impact of these groups are seldom made simply by thoughtful consideration of research evidence. One's judgment of groups, like one's judgment about the behavioral approach described in Chapter Two, depends in part on one's other values. Since these groups represent spontaneity, freedom, and intimacy, they are likely to be rejected to the extent that society is inhibited, individualistic, and impersonal. How can the tension between such sets of values be resolved? "I suggest only that concepts such as the reification of openness and honesty, the celebration of the body, and regard for one's inner experiences deserve no less respect than the set which urges the benefits of self-denial, self-discipline, and self-mastery as prerequisites to the joys of competence, intellectual achievement, and productivity" (Parloff, 1970, p. 301).

Rogers puts the matter more directly. He describes groups as helping people become more spontaneous, flexible, closely related to their feelings, open to their experience, and closer and more expressively intimate in their interpersonal relationships.

If we value this type of behavior, then clearly the group process is a valuable process. If, on the other hand, we place a value on the individual who is effective in suppressing his feelings, who operates from a firm set of principles, who does not trust his own reactions and experience but relies on authority, who remains aloof in his interpersonal relationships, then we would regard the group process . . . as a dangerous force. Clearly there is room for a difference of opinion on this value question and not everyone in our culture would give the same answer [quoted in Gustaitis, 1969, pp. 215–216].

MUTUAL-AID AND SELF-HELP GROUPS

Nearly everyone has heard of Alcoholics Anonymous, but fewer people know how it was established. In 1935 two men met in Akron, Ohio. Dr. Bob was an Akron surgeon, and Bill W. was a stockbroker from New York. Both had been hopeless alcoholics.

In Bill, Dr. Bob found a fellow sufferer who had controlled his alcoholism. They shared their stories with others. Soon a group was formed in Cleveland and another in New York. The movement took root during the early forties and has grown to involve hundreds of thousands of people in thousands of groups throughout the United States and Canada. Both Dr. Bob and Bill W. had experienced the practice of confession as members of religious groups. They introduced secularized versions of confession and other religious practices into A.A. Members confessed that they had problems with drink, told their personal life stories to one another, exhorted one another to live right and to follow religious precepts (as each person understood religion), and offered mutual support during times of temptation.

As the movement grew in numbers and experience, certain principles emerged as basic beliefs. Some of these were concerned primarily with organizational matters and, in 1950, a dozen of them were endorsed as the "Twelve Traditions of Alcoholics Anonymous" (Anonymous, 1953).

1. Our common welfare should come first; personal recovery depends upon A.A. unity.
2. For our group purpose there is but one ultimate authority—a loving God as He may express Himself in our group conscience. Our leaders are but trusted servants; they do not govern.
3. The only requirement for A.A. membership is a desire to stop drinking.
4. Each group should be autonomous except in matters affecting other groups or A.A. as a whole.
5. Each group has but one primary purpose—to carry its message to the alcoholic who still suffers.

6.   An A.A. group ought never endorse, finance or lend the A.A. name to any related facility or outside enterprise lest problems of money, property, and prestige divert us from our primary purpose.
7.   Every A.A. group ought to be fully self-supporting, declining outside contributions.
8.   Alcoholics Anonymous should remain forever nonprofessional, but our service centers may employ special workers.
9.   A.A. as such ought never to be organized; but we may create service boards or committees directly responsible to those they serve.
10.   Alcoholics Anonymous has no opinion on outside issues; hence the A.A. name ought never to be drawn into public controversy.
11.   Our public relations policy is based on attraction rather than promotion; we need always maintain the personal anonymity at the level of press, radio and films.
12.   Anonymity is the spiritual foundation of our traditions, ever reminding us to place principles before personalities.

Why do alcoholics respond to A.A.? One important factor is the credibility of an alcoholic who no longer drinks in reaching and helping the uncontrolled drinker. Hearing how others overcame their problems, seeing how they continue to support one another, and feeling that support —these factors give strength to one who has admitted but not conquered alcoholism. Members assert that only the problem drinker can determine the seriousness of the problem and express a willingness to change. The path to recovery is described in A.A.'s "Twelve Suggested Steps" (Anonymous, 1953), of which the first is an admission of powerlessness:

1.   We admitted we were powerless over alcohol—that our lives had become unmanageable.
2.   Came to believe that a Power greater than ourselves could restore us to sanity.
3.   Made a decision to turn our will and our lives over to the care of God as we understood Him.
4.   Made a searching and fearless moral inventory of ourselves.
5.   Admitted to God, to ourselves, and to another human being, the exact nature of our wrongs.
6.   Were entirely ready to have God remove all these defects of character.
7.   Humbly asked Him to remove our shortcomings.
8.   Made a list of all the persons we had harmed, and became willing to make amends to them all.
9.   Made direct amends to such people wherever possible, except when to do so would injure them or others.
10.   Continued to take personal inventory and when we were wrong, promptly admitted it.

11. Sought through prayer and meditation to improve our conscious contract with God as we understood Him, praying only for knowledge of His will for us and the power to carry that out.
12. Having had a spiritual awakening as the result of these steps, we tried to carry this message to alcoholics and to practice these principles in all our affairs.

Religious notions are prominent in that list, although no orthodoxy of religious belief or practice is imposed on members.

Alcoholics Anonymous illustrates a number of characteristics common to mutual-aid and self-help groups. The remainder of this chapter will discuss several organizational principles and several psychological principles that describe and explain the remarkable growth and success of these groups, many of which are expressly built on the precedent of A.A.

Organizational principles.   Most mutual-aid and self-help groups reflect the following five organizational principles (adapted from Borman, personal communication):

1. Common experience among members.   The initial reason for forming a group is an experience or problem that sets the members apart from others. The group is a place to share that experience and to seek change both in themselves and in social conditions.

Here are a few of the hundreds of mutual-aid and self-help organizations around the United States:

Alanon and Alateen (families of alcoholics)
Committee to Combat Huntington's Disease
Fortune Society (ex-convicts)
Gambler's Anonymous
Little People of America (dwarfs and other undersized persons)
Mended Hearts, Inc. (heart surgery)
Neurotics Anonymous
Parents Anonymous (child abusers)
Parents without Partners (single parents)
Reach to Recovery (mastectomy)
Recovery, Inc. (former mental patients)
Stroke Club
Synanon (drug addicts)
TOPS (Take Off Pounds Sensibly)
Weight Watchers International

Add to this list the consciousness-raising groups for homosexuals, women, ethnic minorities, welfare recipients, and so on, and the tremendous scope of this movement becomes apparent. There is great variety among groups, and there is great commonality within groups. "Their membership consists of those who share a common condition, situation, heritage, symptom, or experience" (Borman, 1975, p. vi).

Society tends to diagnose, stigmatize, and segregate these people. Many groups are initially organized as a defense against society's label of "deviant." After all, who wants to deal sympathetically with a child abuser —except a former child abuser? "One of the most fundamental issues involved in self-help by stigmatized individuals is that those who experience the condition perceive and define it differently than does the prevailing society" (Traunstein & Steinman, 1973, p. 231). So people similarly stigmatized find and help one another.

Groups differ, however, in the ways they seek to deal with what originally brought them together. On the one hand, members of A.A. seek to change their behavior to accommodate to the norms of society. On the other hand, members of the Mattachine Society, an organization of homosexuals, seek to change the norms of society to accommodate their behavior (Sagarin, 1969).

2. Self-government. Mutual-aid groups are governed by their membership. While this may seem circular—the people receiving services are those who also make policy about the service—it is essential to success. Ordinarily recipients of, say, social-welfare programs have little influence on those programs. Hence there are frustrations caused by the bureaucracy's lack of responsiveness. When the recipients of service also set and administer policy, such frustrations should be minimized. Consequently, mutual-aid groups are not led by experts in therapy. They are staffed not by professional administrators, but by experts in the condition of members, those who have already dealt personally with the issue around which the group was formed. Members are seldom referred to professionals, since what members need is better provided by experts who are members of the group.

3. Consensual decision making. Policy making by an elite minority tends to fragment a group. A powerful means for increasing cohesion and solidarity is to involve all members in decision making, and groups are able to do this if they are relatively small. For organizations with an extensive history, such as A.A., much policy has already been formed. Remaining decisions can then be made by consensus.

4. Financial self-sufficiency. Fees for most mutual-aid groups are modest, and expenses are minimal, since the organizational structure is not elaborate. Dues and contributions are usually sufficient to balance the budget. Some groups have branched into commercial ventures—books, foods, and the consequent advertising in the case of Weight Watchers— but most depend on free publicity based on merit. Some feel that financial profit might corrupt their effectiveness and have shunned grants or large donations. A.A. has enforced a limit of $300 on donations and thereby rejected several large bequests of money and property. The groups seek success in converting and changing individuals; they do not measure their success by the usual materialistic criteria.

5. *Identifiable code of precepts and practices.*   As we have seen with A.A., some groups have codified their guides for organizational and individual conduct. Some have fairly specific and elaborate criteria for membership eligibility and responsibility.

Groups have developed rituals (to be discussed below) that become part of their tradition and use slogans that add to the group's traditions. "You alone can do it, but you cannot do it alone" is a slogan used in several groups. It nicely expresses the required simultaneous reliance on oneself and on others. Members must believe in both the necessity and the insufficiency of self-determination.

Psychological principles.   We now move from the organizations to the experience of individuals. I believe there are at least four features that make a significant psychological contribution to the success of these groups. They are personal responsibility, confession and honesty, ritual, and action.

1. *Personal responsibility.*   Before anything can be accomplished in a group, the prospective member must admit a problem that is personally unsolvable. Recall the first of the Alcoholics Anonymous Twelve Steps: "We admitted we were powerless over alcohol—that our lives had become unmanageable." The member must also acknowledge that ultimately only he or she can take responsibility for solving the problem. Here again is the paradox "You alone can do it, but you cannot do it alone." Members know that the group *can* help but that any individual who fails to work on a cure is not worth the group's effort. "We carry the message, not the alcoholic," say A.A. members.

Rationalizations are unacceptable in these groups. Fat may not be explained away by glandular activity nor alcoholism by a broken home. Drug addiction is not maintained because of a deprived childhood, nor does marital distrust continue because "we never could communicate well." Undesirable behavior patterns persist until the individual, supported by the group, adopts new patterns of action.

At Synanon houses, for example, new residents are pressured to assume responsibility. The addict needs no sympathy, it is believed, because sympathy permits rationalization of the addiction. And so in "attack therapy" Synanon members use language that is cold and hard.

> You stupid slob—you've run yourself into the ground by your behavior. Your tough-guy-dope-fiend style keeps getting you dropped off

in a cage. You're not really bad; you're just stupid and ridiculous. Look at how ridiculous you are: like a rat, you ran up and down alleys stealing; you buy some white powder, and then you jam a needle with some fluid in your arm, conk out, and go back for more. Of course, you are killing yourself. You will either die by being locked up for life or die from an overdose in a back alley. Your *behavior* is ridiculous! [Yablonsky, 1965, p. 384].

Considerable affection and support are given at Synanon, but there is universal distaste for a resident's former life and behavior: it is despicable, it is no one's fault but that person's, and only with the group's help can it be changed.

Pressure to admit responsibility continues in the "Synanon game," several intense hours of frequent shouting and screaming, often with psychic (but not physical) violence aimed at a particular group member. The session might proceed something like this: After dividing into game groups and some initial chatter, a member begins with a sharp blast aimed at a man in the group. Another member, a woman, jumps in with a critical observation about him and the game begins. The group attack is brutal, touching on many problems besides drug addiction, until the man is "pinned to the wall" and begins making excuses for his weak behavior and his failure to stop being bored and fulfill a dream that he quit accounting and enter law school. When he uses the excuse of gambling debts to postpone changing his life style, the group brings his procrastination and his reluctance to change into sharp focus. He will never stop gambling because it protects him from reaching his dreams. When the game turns to another man, his drinking is exposed as the crutch he uses to delay the realization of his dreams to get married. No play for sympathy, no reason not to change, no plea for mercy is left unexamined in the crucible of the Synanon game (Gustaitis, 1969).

Some professionals consider such apparently unsupportive "therapy" to be extremely dangerous. In many helping groups the preference is to exert no pressure and to wait until a new member chooses to take responsibility. Yet for Synanon, at least, the game seems to work, perhaps because it is part of a larger supportive program. Clearly, the game discourages rationalizing and illustrates Synanon's insistence on individual responsibility.

2. Confession and honesty. Group members are encouraged to be frank and honest about their problems. Sharing helps to solidify the group. Members can learn that others accept them even when they feel they have revealed disgraceful and hidden parts of their lives. Most groups have closed meetings and impose a bond of privacy so that what is said there goes no further.

Even when the problem is obvious to all the world—obesity, for example—privacy of the group is important. One person begins to talk, then another, and finally all are relieving the burden of their problem with others who understand.

> The biggest reason Weight Watchers is such a success is that fat people can finally talk freely, openly and honestly. We can reveal our real feelings to other people and those other people will understand. I can say to a Weight Watchers class, "I remember sitting in a bathtub watching my fat floating," and there isn't a person here who can't relate to me at that moment. A thin person would never understand that [Nidetch, 1970, p. 18].

Confession is a significant component of Integrity Groups, an approach developed by psychologist O. Hobart Mowrer. During weekly small-group meetings, members reveal aspects of their lives that are examined in light of Integrity Groups' basic principles: honesty, responsibility, and involvement. If a member confesses something that has been guilt producing, confession may counteract the guilt. Other members then assist in planning how to confess to "significant others" beyond the group.

An episode from one Integrity Group reported by Mowrer (1972) serves as an example. During an initial intake interview for the Integrity Group, Madeline had said she was hiding nothing from her husband. But in response to a question by another group member, "What do you regard as the worst thing you have ever done in your life?" she told the story of having represented herself as a virgin to her husband when in fact she had met him on the rebound from an extended affair. She wanted to be sure her husband would never be in the group or find out about her confession. However, after making this confession to the group, she felt considerable internal pressure to do something about the situation before she faced the group at the next session. And so she told her husband how she had lied to him, and that she might not even have married him if the situation had been different. Because of the group's expectations, Madeline had become more honest not only with group members but also with her husband.

Later Richard (her husband) joined the group. He confessed an incident with a prostitute during a low point in their marriage and further revealed that long ago friends of his had told him of Madeline's affair.

> Thus, all along, Richard had "had something" on his wife and was in a sense silently "blackmailing" her with it—or at least using it to rationalize some of his own less-than-perfect behavior, including the incident with the prostitute. But Madeline had had the character to be severely uncomfortable about the incompleteness and dishonesty in her relationship with Richard. And when, in the context of our

Integrity Groups, she had a chance to really clear the whole thing up, she threw Richard badly off balance, and he was beginning to look at himself as the "heel" he really was, rather than secretly capitalizing upon his wife's moral inadequacies. This seemed to put the proper words on Richard's feelings, and he saw the picture "like it was" [Mowrer, 1972, p. 29].

Of course, such relationships are even more tangled and complex than this description conveys, and much remained to be worked out. Nevertheless the couple had at least laid a basis for a more open marriage and in the context of the group could make commitments to sustain their honesty. Consonant with the purposes of the group, their confession had brought them to a new level of integrity.

3. Ritual. Not surprisingly, practices have emerged that symbolize the purposes of particular groups and strengthen the identification of members with the group. Synanon has its game. Integrity Groups have a Commitment Book in which members write their plans for changed behavior.

At A.A., speakers often begin their remarks with a statement such as "My name is ——————. I am an alcoholic. I had my last drink on ——————. By the grace of God and following the program and with the help of A.A., I have managed to stay sober." Some members can say to the day, and do each time they speak at a meeting, how long they have been sober. The sobriety anniversary is of great importance and in some groups is celebrated once each month for all whose sobriety birthday falls in that month. There is birthday cake for all (Drakeford, 1969).

Weight Watchers meetings are also ritualized. First the members check in at the door and pay their weekly fee. Then they are each weighed privately and told today's weight. The amount lost or gained since the previous week is recorded on a weight card. After weighing in, members gather to listen to the lecturer, who talks both personally and in general about weight loss and its problems. Pictures (before and after) are passed around. Ground rules of the diet program are reviewed. Then the lecturer receives the weight cards, calls each person's name, and announces the amount of weight lost or gained. If members wish to make a statement or ask a question, they may do so as names are called. Whenever a Weight Watcher member reaches goal weight, he or she is awarded a pin and lifetime membership dues free, as long as goal weight is maintained (Nidetch, 1970).

These rituals strengthen group ties and increase mutual support. Without them, many people would probably fail to continue to work on their problems.

4. Action. All these groups aim ultimately at changes in individual behavior, and it is true that the ability to act on one's problem is enhanced by first admitting responsibility and then confessing weaknesses. Self-help programs invariably use group pressure to influence behavior.

The new members of Weight Watchers must first observe the diet. Then group support is given for both the changed behavior and the emotional components of attempting a weight change.

Synanon's attack therapy goads members into acting differently. "The underlying assumption is that people mature psychologically after a sufficient period of constructive behavior. In short, positive behavior eventually affects internal psychological adjustment. This process reverses the usual professional approach" (Yablonsky, 1965, p. 192).

Integrity Group literature says that to live a normal integrated existence a person must act on shortcomings in order to remove them. After confession there must be action in the form of changed behavior. The effects of wrongdoing and guilt are counteracted by action. Good feelings come after good actions; comfort comes from effort.

Members of A.A. recognize the need for action to set things right with one's fellows. Recall that three of the Twelve Steps are: "Made a list of all the persons we had harmed, and became willing to make amends to them all." "Made direct amends to such people whenever possible, except when to do so would injure them or others." "Continued to take personal inventory and when we were wrong, promptly admitted it."

Considerable discipline is involved in the activities of group members as they make progress. Of course they abstain from whatever substances and avoid whatever circumstances are related to their problem. Further, they regularly attend meetings and counsel new and prospective members. Indeed, many members show an all-absorbing interest in the activities of the group, at least for a time after they join.

EFFECTIVENESS OF MUTUAL-AID AND SELF-HELP GROUPS

What can be said about the effectiveness of mutual-aid and self-help groups? The answer, of course, depends on the kind of evidence one finds acceptable. Verified testimonials are numerous, and such anecdotes are by far the most common evidence (Hurvitz, 1974). They demonstrate without a doubt that some people change dramatically while participating in a group. However, testimonials do not identify the reasons for change, and they ignore those who do not change. Questionnaire and interview studies—only a few of which have been done—are useful for drawing very broad conclusions. A 1968 survey done at 466 A.A. meetings had 11,355 individual respondents. Of these, 64% reported that they had stopped drinking, either immediately after their first meeting (41%) or within the first year (23%). An additional 18% stopped within two to five years. Of those surveyed, 95% indicated that they attend at least one meeting a week. But A.A. dropouts (failures) are not identified by such a survey, because many of them obviously no longer attend meetings (Menges & Pennington, 1971).

Synanon claims 40–60% recovery rates, compared with 1–4% in federal-hospital addiction programs (Hurvitz, 1974). Integrity Groups research includes several studies that document positive changes in personality profiles as a result of group participation. Unfortunately, members of some groups hold a bias against research. They suspect researchers of serving their own interests rather than the interests of the group and of using methods that interfere with the group process. Consequently, the dynamics of these groups are no better understood than are the dynamics of encounter and sensitivity groups.

Some professionals, perhaps spitefully, have attacked such groups as nothing more than fads, cults, or contemporary substitutes for religion. Hurvitz (1970) summarizes the attacks on A.A. that call it a "substitute for mother" and on the charisma of Chuck Dederich, Synanon's founder. Such attacks are not likely to be fruitful, since they fail to explain how the groups produce their successes. My own speculation is that these groups work in the main because of the concern and support they show for the troubled person. This process may be similar to the placebo effect. In medical research, subjects have been known to improve even though they were given inert "medication" (the placebo); apparently the attention and expectations involved in being "in treatment" actually aided in recovery. Something similar may happen in peer and self-help groups: general group support may be more important than features peculiar to a particular group. Perhaps systematic analysis and research will identify how this general effect occurs and what other effects may be at work. Until then, we would do well to exploit the powerful effects of group concern and mutual support.

THE HELPING ROLE IN TEACHING AND LEARNING

The teacher's helping role creates a paradox. On the one hand, virtually everyone who attempts to facilitate learning in others thinks of teachers as helpers. On the other hand, formal education provides few opportunities for the explicit attention to the development and expression of feelings that is the essence of helping. We have considered a number of helping activities that at first seem unrelated to the typical context of teaching and learning. In this section, the actual relationships are explored in detail.

The teacher who wishes to be a helper does not pose as a counselor or as a therapist. The teacher's business is not primarily personality growth or adjustment counseling; it is the facilitation of learning. Learning, in the broad sense, is precisely what encounter groups, training groups, and mutual-aid groups facilitate. The trained Weight Watchers lecturer is indeed a teacher, as are encounter-group or training-group leaders. While these activities require sensitivity to therapeutic concerns, they do not require that the leader be trained as a therapist or counselor. In short, they may be regarded primarily as teaching/learning activities.

Other helping skills are useful for teachers in settings where the main goal is subject-matter learning as well as in settings where explicit attention to feelings is considered important. The ability to communicate clearly and to deal appropriately with the feeling component of communication is central to life success. Consider the number of significant personal and occupational activities in which the primary effort is communicating with people rather than dealing with ideas or manipulating objects. Using I-messages, responding with empathy, and displaying other skills fostered by the helping teacher are useful in all those communication situations.

Each of the activities described here should be analyzed to identify the learning principles at work so that those principles may be applied in other settings. In particular, the success of mutual-aid groups should be investigated and experimented with in schools. A school that attempts to apply mutual-aid principles might encourage students to form learning and growth groups based on common experiences and problems. The groups would be largely self-governing and would attempt to foster open and honest communication. Members would be held responsible for their actions, and the group would support individual members' personal learning and growth projects. Rituals and ceremonies might evolve as ways of expressing the group's solidarity.

Teachers who attempt to carry out the helping role in conventional classrooms express personal feelings and acknowledge the feelings expressed by others. They attempt to foster group consensus in decision making. They trust the wisdom of decisions made by the group to the extent of letting students experience the consequences of those decisions.

I believe that the values expressed by such activities are good in themselves and need no further justification. Nevertheless, it is true that the climate fostered by the teacher as helper is an important vehicle for subject-matter learning. Cognitive learning is enhanced when teachers are perceived as warm, when student groups are cohesive, and when the institutional climate is supportive (Napier, Hayman, & Moskowitz, 1976). These desirable characteristics of the learning environment are more likely to emerge when there is attention to feelings and to hunches—to all the expressions of tentativeness discussed in this chapter.

FOR FURTHER READING

Encounter and Training Groups

A very thoughtful study of the group phenomenon, interestingly titled *Beyond Words,* is provided by Back (1973). Menges and McGaghie (1974) discuss the distinctiveness of interpersonal learning and list some categories by which it may be evaluated.

In addition to the novels mentioned in the chapter, there are several nonfiction accounts of experience in a variety of encounter and training groups. Especially helpful are *Face to Face: The Small Group Experience and Interpersonal Growth* (Egan, 1973); *Please Touch: A Guided Tour of the Human Potential Movement* (Howard, 1970); *The Shared Journey: An Introduction to Encounter* (O'Banion & O'Connell, 1970); and *Carl Rogers on Encounter Groups* (Rogers, 1970).

Guide books of encounter-like activities include *Growth Games: How to Tune in Yourself, Your Family, Your Friends* (Lewis & Streitfeld, 1972) and *Reality Games* (Sax & Hollander, 1972).

National Training Labs program information and schedules may be obtained from NTL Institute, Box 9155, Rosslyn Station, Arlington, Virginia 22209.

Discussions of the motive to achieve and of programs designed to enhance that motive can be found in *Developing Achievement Motivation in Adolescents* (Alschuler, 1973); "From Pawns to Origins" (De Charms, 1971); and *Sociocultural Origins of Achievement* (Maehr, 1974).

Mutual-Aid and Self-Help Groups

Highly readable sources describing several of the organizations discussed in this chapter are *Farewell to the Lonely Crowd* (Drakeford, 1969); *Turning On* (Gustaitis, 1969); *Odd Man In: Societies of Deviants in America* (Sagarin, 1969); and *The Strength in Us: Self-Help Groups in the Modern World* (Katz & Bender, 1976).

A more technical comparison of such groups with psychotherapy is provided by Hurvitz (1974), "Peer Self-Help Psychotherapy Groups: Psychotherapy without Psychotherapists."

The Helping Role in Teaching and Learning

In *Classroom Dynamics: Viewing the Classroom as a Social System,* Napier, Hayman, and Moskowitz (1976) discuss theory and research on group cohesion, warmth, and other variables.

Some of the principles of mutual aid groups have been applied to a college course by Bassin (1974) in "The Therapeutic Community Teaching Concept in Behavioral Science Education."

CHAPTER
FIVE

THE INTENTIONAL TEACHER

The notion of the intentional teacher accomodates many important concepts related to the teaching-learning process. It views teaching as an art but does not ignore the particular skills of teaching. It includes teaching as a profession and teaching as a craft. It emphasizes personal and uniquely human qualities of the teacher and the learner as well as characteristics of the subject matter. It suits a wide variety of roles such as the three roles of controller, manager, and helper.

In this chapter I shall describe work that deals explicitly with intention and that expands our view of persons as intentional individuals. I shall attempt to relate this work to the roles of teachers discussed in previous chapters and suggest ways of increasing intentionality. First, it is helpful to examine variables other than intentions that have claimed the efforts of those who investigate the determinants of human behavior.

WHY DO PEOPLE DO WHAT THEY DO?

Much theory and research has been directed in one way or another toward this fundamental question: Why do people do what they do? The search for variables that will enable us to understand and perhaps to predict human behavior has followed many paths and proposed many answers.

One answer to the question is that people do what they *know*. According to this view, behavior is primarily determined by the individual's knowledge and belief. Determinants of behavior are cognitive and intellectual, the very faculties that are uniquely developed in humans.

A second answer is that people do what they *like*. Behavioral determinants in this view range from what feels good (hedonism) to what coincides with one's attitudes. They share a concern with affect, and their primary component is feeling rather than thought.

A third answer says that people do what they *can*. This view examines skills of various sorts in order to determine whether the desired behaviors are in a person's repertoire. Since a person will not do what he or she cannot do, establishing a relevant repertoire of skills is a necessary prerequisite to appropriate behavior.

According to a fourth view, people do what they *must*. This view is deterministic and may emphasize biological, social, or psychological determinism. Determinism is basic to behavioral psychology, which holds that knowledge of a person's biological constitution and reinforcement history is sufficient for predicting that person's future behavior. Determinism is also basic to Freudian psychoanalysis, which holds that instinctual forces and unconscious needs determine behavior. These deterministic forces are said to operate quite independently of the person's knowledge, attitudes, and skills.

A final answer is that people do what they *intend*. According to this view, particular behavior is deliberate and is chosen from a range of available alternatives. Intentions, if adequate, comprehend the person's knowledge, attitudes, skills, and needs, and this comprehensive nature of intention is its great advantage. Intentions reflect both the general disposition of an individual (a teacher may be more comfortable as a helper, say, than as a controller) and the demands of a particular situation (the teacher's specific instructional task). Work to be reviewed below shows how needs, skills, beliefs, and attitudes are all embraced by the intentional individual's behavior. I believe that this view of human nature and behavior is held by most people, although they may not express it as do the scholars whose positions we consider in this chapter.

THE DISCREPANCY BETWEEN INTENTION AND BEHAVIOR

I am at war with myself: what I want to do,
I don't do; what I don't want to do, I do.—Romans 7:19

Imagine two balloon-like spheres. Imagine further that their membranes are such that one of them can partially or completely merge with the other. One sphere is the totality of one's intentions; the other sphere is the totality of one's behaviors. To the extent that these two are congruent, to the extent that a person's intention and behavior spheres have merged, that person is an intentional individual.

Can the merger ever be complete? The extent of intentionality depends first of all on whether every element in the sphere of behavior has a counterpart in the sphere of intention. Some behavior seems not to be the result of deliberate choice, conscious or unconscious. Physiological functions of the body, for example, are automatic; while we can learn to control some of them (if we intend to do so), they will operate quite well without our intervention. So we must conclude that there is indeed some be-havior without intention.

The other side of our question about intention-behavior congru-ence is this: Is there intention without behavior? The lives of most of us provide considerable evidence that there is. "I intend to study but am watch-ing television instead." "I intend to be more thorough in planning assign-ments for my classes but spend all evening finishing these attendance re-ports." "I intend to spend more time with my children but am going to meetings every night this week."

The actual behavior of classroom teachers is often quite different from the behavior they say they intend. Recall that an earlier chapter cited research showing that most teachers from kindergarten through high school were more negative than positive in their dealings with students. Only 8% of the thousands of teachers studied gave more approval (for appropriate behavior) than disapproval (for inappropriate social be-havior). Yet on questionnaires nearly every one of them agreed that the classroom environment should be positive and that comments of an ap-proving nature by the teacher would indicate a positive environment (Madsen & Madsen, 1974). Apparently their intention was to be positive, but their behavior was negative.

In other research, teachers have been asked to estimate the fre-quency of particular classroom behaviors. Those estimates are then com-pared with records made by classroom observers. Estimates made by stu-dents usually agree with the estimates of trained observers; estimates by teachers usually do not. For example, teachers consistently underestimate the amount of talking they do in the class. They also tend to overestimate the number of opportunities students have for making decisions in the classroom. (These and related findings are described by Good & Brophy, 1973.)

Inaccurate estimates by teachers are quite understandable. The complexity of classroom events is such that full concentration by trained observers is necessary to record them adequately. Whatever the reason, discrepancies remain between intention and action. The congruence is never perfect because some behaviors have no corresponding intentions, and because no one is likely to realize every intention in behavior. In the next section, some additional aspects of intentions as determinants of be-havior are presented.

THREE VIEWS OF INTENTIONS

An interest in the topic of intention can be found in quite diverse approaches to the study of human behavior. Three contributions are de-scribed here—one from the perspective of psychoanalysis, one from the tradition of social psychology, and one from behavioral psychology.

A VIEW FROM PSYCHOANALYSIS

Freudian psychology is a system based on determinism. According to this system, behavior is determined by psychic forces, often deriving from early childhood experiences. A person may become more aware of these forces through the psychoanalytic process, which aims at making the unconscious conscious. The patient may then feel more free and more able to choose from behavioral alternatives. But that feeling of freedom is illusory, since in a deterministic system the freedom to change cannot be real. Thus the psychoanalyst, at least the Freudian psychoanalyst, encourages not the pursuit of truth but pursuit of an illusion.

Rollo May, a psychoanalyst, deals with this paradox in his book *Love and Will* (1969), and this section traces part of the argument he develops in Chapters Seven through Ten of that book. First, he deals with the issues of determinism and freedom. He notes that the consciousness possessed by human beings alters what might otherwise be a highly predictable (determined) system. Further, he contends that complete determinism is self-contradictory, in that the very raising of questions about determinism demonstrates an element of freedom. There would be no need to demonstrate complete determinism, or to attempt to refute it, if it were true. May does not deny significant determinism—the operation of unconscious forces, for example; he merely denies *complete* determinism.

It is this very acknowledgement of unconscious forces that is an important contribution of psychoanalysis to the understanding of intentions. May reminds us that no intention is entirely conscious. There are always aspects beyond awareness that would enrich the intention and make it more realizable. The tools of psychoanalysis help to reveal those unconscious aspects. In seeking to clarify an intention, for example, a psychoanalytic patient may use free association. Saying whatever occurs to one may add to the breadth of one's intention and increase the likelihood of its becoming action. Cultivation of the imagination (the ability to "image") may also enrich intentions. May speaks of "wish" as preceeding "will." "Wish is the imaginative playing with the possibility of some act. . . . Will is the capacity to organize oneself [for movement or change]" (1969, p. 218).

To accommodate these unconscious aspects, May offers the term *intentionality* and distinguishes it from intention. Intentionality is a structure underlying intentions, a capacity to have intentions. But it is never solely conscious.

Part of the word *intention* ("tend") means a turning toward, a looking ahead. It is not just a push from the past or an influence from the intellect. The multiple meanings of the term *will* also imply a future orientation. Another etymological fact about *intention*, also noted by May, is that the first meaning of intend in Webster's is "to mean, signify." Only second is "to have in mind a purpose or design" given as a meaning. Bringing these strands together, we see that intention implies a turning toward something (an act) that is already meaningful. Behavior cannot be understood apart from intention, and intention is already turning toward behavior.

Because separating intent and act seems so natural to us, this point is an especially difficult one. Since Descartes, at least, we have been thinking dualistically, conceiving of everything as either subject or object. Thinking of intention and behavior as separate spheres exemplifies that dualism, and so we find it extraordinary when intention and behavior are congruent. May reminds us that in truth intention and action are inseparable and that what is extraordinary is their separation. "The act is in the intention, and the intention in the act" (1969, p. 242).

These psychoanalytic views assist our understanding of intention by reminding us of the untiy of thought, will, and action. If in fact we observe a divorce between intent and behavior ("I want to stop smoking, but just can't"), May's position implies two things: first, that the intention may not yet be adequately clarified, that its tendencies and implications may need further development; second, that psychoanalytic methods may be useful in improving the clarity of that intention by providing access to related nonconscious material.

A VIEW FROM SOCIAL PSYCHOLOGY

Researchers trained in experimental social psychology view intention as an estimate of the likelihood of behavior. What are the chances from a person's point of view that he or she will perform a particular action? That subjective probability refers to the person's intention. (This definition and much of the following material draws upon Fishbein & Ajzen, 1975, particularly Chapters Seven and Eight.)

To determine the adequacy with which intentions predict behavior, a researcher gathers the individual's subjective probability estimate and compares it with observed behavior. Fortunately, the method for identifying intentions is quite straightforward: Just ask. To measure intentions about voting behavior, for example, the following is an appropriate question: "If the election were tomorrow and candidates X and Y were running, for whom would you vote?" Answers to such questions are usually highly congruent with self-reports of subsequent behavior (assuming both are honest). If time intervenes between the question and the vote, accuracy of prediction decreases, because new information and experience may alter the intention, which in turn alters the behavior.

How then do we interpret an unrealized intention, an intention, say, to reduce calorie intake? The social-psychology view assumes that at the moment of eating a forbidden dessert the intention, if honestly reported, would in fact be congruent with the behavior, because the intention would have changed. That is, the person would now say "I intend to eat that dessert."

To be confident of a close relationship between intention and behavior, we must also assume that the behavior is potentially within the individual's volitional control. It should not be outside the range of ability, as straight A's for a retarded child would be. It should not lie outside the range of opportunity, as heterosexual intercourse for a prisoner probably would. Nor should it involve automatic behaviors such as habitual typing errors.

So far this view seems to have added little of value to our understanding of intention. Perhaps all we have done is define and measure intention in a way that guarantees a high correlation with behavior. It would be much more useful if intentions helped us to *understand* behavior, not merely to predict it. And so we move the question back one step: What are the determinants of the intention? Knowing them would help us to understand behavior.

The research of Fishbein and Ajzen supports a model of intention formation that has two components. Intention with regard to a particular behavior $(B \sim I)$ is a function of (1) attitude toward performing that behavior (A_B) and (2) belief about the views of others toward that behavior (SN). Each component has a weight in a given instance $(w_1$ or $w_2)$. The summarizing equation is as follows (Fishbein & Ajzen, 1975, p. 301):

$$B \sim I = (A_B)w_1 + (SN)w_2$$

Let us examine the two components of this equation in more detail. A_B is the actor's attitude toward performing the behavior in question. What determines this attitude? The actor is presumed to go through a psychological process of estimating the consequences of performing the behavior and then weighing the advantages and disadvantages of doing it in a particular situation. If the advantages are perceived as appropriate, the resulting attitude is positive. If the disadvantages are perceived as greater than the advantages, the attitude is negative.

The second component is SN, the subjective norm. This component is normative and social, in that it deals with the perceived opinions of persons who are important to the actor. Further, this component is a belief rather than an attitude (and is therefore formed differently, as Fishbein and Ajzen discuss in detail). The subjective norm involves the actor's belief that those people who are important with regard to this particular behavior would or would not support the behavior. This belief is affected by a motivational factor—that is, by how strongly the actor wishes to comply with each significant person. Obviously, the importance of this normative component varies with the privacy of the behavior. The motivational element in particular may have almost no influence on the intention to vote for a particular candidate—for example, if no one else is likely to learn for whom the vote was cast.

How might this model illustrate the formation of a particular intention? Harold's intention to apply to law school, for example, is a function first of all of his attitude toward the behavior (A_B). If he applies he may be accepted or rejected. If accepted, how would he feel? If rejected, how would he feel? How does applying to more than one law school change the likely outcomes? In short, what is his *attitude* toward the behavior of applying?

Second, what is the relevant subjective norm (SN)? What does Harold perceive to be the reaction of family, friends, and society at large? How strongly motivated is he to comply with each of these perceived reactions? In short, what does he *believe* about others' views of this behavior, and how important does he consider their views to be?

This social-psychological model and its supporting research evidence illuminate our understanding of intention in three ways. First, it separates the contributions of attitudes and beliefs. Attitudes are important in A_B; beliefs are important in SN. Second, it emphasizes social influence (the subjective norm) as an influence on intention. Finally, with additional research I believe it will show how intentions are altered. There is already some suggestion (Fishbein & Ajzen, 1975) that attitudes toward a particular behavior (A_B) may be altered in carefully designed situations. If Harold were to role play a situation in which he received a letter of rejection from law school, he might change his perception of the consequences of applying to law school. The subjective norm, on the other hand, may be altered by new information. Data on lawyer's salaries projected over the next decade may alter his subjective norms if he prizes the company of high-salaried colleagues.

A VIEW FROM BEHAVIORAL PSYCHOLOGY

In an earlier chapter we reviewed the major principles and some educational applications of behavioral psychology. A number of programs in teacher education and counselor education are attempting to combine behavioral contributions with the traditionally humanistic concern for maximizing the unique aspects of each individual's development. Such programs are using behavioral technology for humanistic ends (Mahoney & Thoresen, 1974).

Explicit concern with intentions characterizes some of this work. For example, Ivey describes the intentional individual as "one who can generate alternative behaviors in a given situation and can 'come at' a problem from different vantage points or theoretical views as he receives environmental feedback. Equally important, the individual who acts with intentionality is not bound to one course of action, but can act 'in the moment' to respond to ever-changing environmental situations" (Ivey, 1969, pp. 57–58).

There are three major elements in this view of the intentional individual. First, the intentional individual possesses an array of skills, a repertoire of behaviors. The individual chooses a skill or skills according to the circumstances of a particular situation and thus forms an intention to perform that act. "Intentionality is the process of fusing conscious consideration of alternatives with positive action" (Alschuler & Ivey, 1972, p. 54). Thus it is not enough merely to possess the skills; one must know the limits of generalizability of each skill in order to choose the one which is most appropriate. The behavioral approach reminds us of the essential need to possess the skill in the first place.

Second, the intentional individual is sensitive to environmental feedback. After an intention is chosen and realized in behavior, what are its consequences? Does the behavior change the environment as the actor expected? If so, it should probably be continued. If not, it should be altered. Utilizing feedback to maintain or modify behavior is essential for actualizing intentions.

The third element is flexibility, the ability to select a new skill on the basis of negative feedback or of changes in the environment. The exercise of intentionality illustrates a feedback model that emphasizes process as much as outcome. Results of intentions are continuously monitored, and feedback suggesting the need for change results in identification of a different skill (or even of a modified intention) and consequently of new behavior.

An illustration of a student teacher demonstrating intentionally is provided by Ivey:

> Susie had a beautiful lesson in human relations. She wanted to share with her fifth grade students some of her ideas about listening to others. She sat on the floor and asked the children to play "gossip" . . . to pass a message around the circle by whispering.
> After the circle had gone around a few times, Susie asked the

children to discuss what had happened. The children engaged in an excellent discussion of how one learns from listening to others. The children continued the discussion on their own and Susie became a participant with them as they explored the topic. As the children became more involved, Susie dropped out of the discussion and became an interested listener. She was particularly pleased when Craig, usually a negative discipline problem, pointed out that "listening is not necessarily hearing" [Ivey, 1969, p. 58].

In this lesson Susie was able to draw upon a variety of skills including attentive listening, discussion leading, discussion participation, and even discussion following. She had a plan for the start of the lesson, but she changed her behavior, and presumably her intentions, according to feedback provided by the children. Because she had a large number of behavioral options in her repertoire, she was able to choose what "felt right" in the moment and observe its consequences.

Educational programs reflecting these views emphasize the acquisition of specific skills. For example, some counselor-education programs require students to demonstrate their competence in listening. Observable behaviors that indicate listening include (1) eye contact, (2) physical attention, and (3) verbal following. It is possible to rate the presence of these behaviors accurately, to provide exercises that increase their frequency, and to demonstrate that they facilitate effectiveness in counseling interviews (Ivey, 1972). A large number of such skills have been identified. Training programs often involve videotape, an excellent source of feedback.

One curriculum in human relations requires trainees to teach their newly acquired skills to others. The curriculum is performance based, in that each trainee moves to new skills upon performing earlier skills, but the trainee must also show insight regarding the appropriate application of the skills. Such a program reflects the behavioral approach in several ways. It emphasizes observable behavior and uses behavioral performance as the criterion of learning. Intentions are not dealt with directly; they are merely inferred from observed behaviors.

The central emphasis on feedback in this model is analogous to the importance of reinforcement in the behavioral approach. But these views go beyond behaviorism by acknowledging decision-making processes that underlie the formation of intentions.

The major contribution of behaviorism to our understanding of intentions is its emphasis on providing a range of skills without which intention would not be possible. Behavioral technology is helpful in identifying such skills and in designing procedures for teaching them.

A PROGRAM FOR INCREASING
INTENTION-BEHAVIOR CONGRUENCE

The preceding chapters have discussed teaching and learning with illustrations from a variety of settings. The notion of intention-behavior congruence is appropriate to all of these settings (classrooms, clinical practice, individual tutoring), to all subject matter (foreign language, calculus, motor skills, communication clarity), and to each of the teacher roles (controller, manager, helper). A reduction of the discrepancy between a teacher's intentions and behavior is most likely under two conditions. The first condition is that the teacher have intentions that are clear and realistic. The second condition is that the teacher have accurate information about his or her behavior and its effects on others. A program for professional self-development can be constructed around activities related to these two conditions, and the remainder of this chapter is devoted to a description of the components of such a program.

TOWARD MORE ADEQUATE INTENTIONS

Efforts at forming clear and realistic intentions may take many directions. At least five components are suggested by material presented earlier in this chapter, and in this section I explore the implications of that material for professional self-development.

Models.   Clarity of intentions is enhanced if the teacher can point to a model of what teaching *should* be. Such a model may be an actual master teacher or a fictional character, or it may be hypothetical. The teacher roles of controller, manager, and helper are hypothetical models. They may be useful as the teacher attempts to discern what each would do in being faithful to that role in a particular situation. Of course, other hypothetical models may be derived logically from theories of teaching and theories of learning. For example, four major types are presented in *Models of Teaching* (Joyce & Weil, 1972): social-interaction models, information-processing models, personal-source models, and behavior-modification models. Each is elaborated in terms of specific subtypes.

Reading about such models and attempting to identify congenial real-life models is interesting as an intellectual exercise, but it is also useful in that it aids the teacher to clarify personal intentions.

Needs and feelings.   The psychoanalytic work on intention is particularly helpful in emphasizing the importance of the teacher's own feelings in distorting or inhibiting the formulation of adequate intentions. Are teacher biases against some children and toward other children due to unconscious needs and feelings? How do teachers' own childhood experiences with authority figures affect their dealings as adults with supervisors and principals and their assertion of authority in evaluating the work of learners? Can these issues be illuminated by the use of psychoanalytic tools such as free association and dream analysis?

These are questions for which I have no ready answers, since personal psychoanalysis for all teachers is impractical. Some of the work can be done in groups of either the encounter or mutual-aid type, but maturity and skill of the group leader are crucial. In any case, the effects of unconscious needs and feelings on intentions are sufficiently important to justify greater attention to this aspect of teachers' development.

Skills.   An intention may be derived initially from a model. It may be analyzed to ensure that it does not reflect undesirable unconscious needs. Next it must be translated into skills. The intention to increase student participation in class discussions, for example, no matter how well clarified, will not be realized in behavior by teachers who do not have the appropriate skills. Behavioral psychology has influenced one approach to teacher education, the performance-based approach, that is very much concerned with specifiable, discrete skills. To increase student participation, the teacher may practice using questions that call for extended answers and giving reinforcement for students who respond to comments of other students, or may reduce the frequency of his or her own comments.

For teachers not engaged in a formal training program, self-instructional materials may be helpful in skill acquisition. An elaborate set of "minicourse" materials has been prepared under government research projects and is distributed by Macmillan Publishing Company. These minicourses include self-instructional manuals, films, and instructions for videotaping one's own classes, redesigning the lesson after reviewing the tape, and reteaching. Minicourse topics include "Effective Questioning (Elementary Level)," "Higher Cognitive Questioning," "Organizing Independent Learning," and "Teaching Reading as Decoding."

Such materials are useful in ensuring that the teacher possesses skills relevant to an intention.

Consequences.   The social-psychological work on intention and behavior change suggests that what one believes about the consequences of performing a behavior is one important component of intentions. Intentions are more likely to become action if the teacher has first worked through the consequences of that action in imagination. One consequence of more student participation in class discussions is a higher level of noise. Teachers may perceive that consequence as so undesirable that they modify the intention. On the other hand, they may find ways to deal with the noise level that permit increased discussions. By playing out in imagination the consequences of the intended action, teachers may strengthen the intention. Discussion with friends and role playing with other teachers may also be helpful. The point is to examine the consequences, because beliefs about consequences affect the attitude about the behavior, which is in turn one determinant of the intention.

Subjective norm. The second determinant of intention from the social-psychological view is the actor's perception of other persons' beliefs regarding the behavior in question. What do the teacher's students, fellow teachers, and administrators in the school believe about increased student participation in discussions? How accurate are the teacher's perceptions of their beliefs?

This subjective norm regarding a particular behavior becomes more accurate as it incorporates objective information. Personal conversations, group discussions, and research reports may all increase the accuracy of a subjective norm. A work setting with open communication patterns is more likely to provide such information than one in which information is conveyed by indirect communication and rumor. In the latter situation, subjective norms may be inaccurate, and consequently intentions may be inappropriate.

In this discussion of the intention side of the intention-behavior discrepancy we have examined five conditions that enhance the adequacy of intentions: clear models from which intentions may be derived, openness to feelings, practice of skills implied by the intention, realization of the consequences of particular behaviors, and accuracy of the subjective norm regarding the behavior. Next we turn to conditions involving the behavior side of the intention-behavior discrepancy.

TOWARD MORE COMPREHENSIVE FEEDBACK

The behavioral model reminds us that, even after an intended behavior is performed, it is necessary to receive feedback so that the intention may be extended or appropriately changed. It is sometimes difficult to know if an intention has the desired effect. How may the adequacy of feedback be increased?

There are three obvious sources of feedback in an instructional situation: oneself, one's students, and a peer observer. Feedback from these sources is usually informal and fragmentary, but there are several ways in which it can be made more systematic.

My intentions for an instructional situation may be formalized by writing down in advance what I intend to accomplish (general goal) and what I will do in order to accomplish it (behavior). Among my specific intentions regarding increasing student discussion, I may aim for speaking less than, say, 25% of the class time, or speaking only one-third as frequently as my students speak. Further, I may distinguish between students' information comments and problem-solving comments, aiming at more of the latter than the former. After class I compare these stated intentions with what actually happened. If I have an audiotape or videotape recording of the class, I can actually count how much student talk and teacher talk occurred, and I can categorize each comment. A colleague observing the class can provide an estimate (or a careful count) of these incidents. I may also ask students to complete a questionnaire that provides their perceptions of what happened.

I now have a statement of my intentions, a taped record of reality (or a colleague's observations), and a record of the perceptions of students. By analyzing and weighing this feedback, I should be able to determine to what extent my intentions were actualized. I may want a trusted colleague to help me to interpret the feedback, but ultimately decisions about subsequent intentions are my own, just as the decisions about original intentions were.

INTENTIONAL TEACHERS ANONYMOUS

Many worthy intentions have remained unactualized for lack of group support. We have seen that the subjective norm is an important factor in intention. Perceived views of significant others are important both in forming intentions and in maintaining required behavior changes. A mutual-aid group would provide a powerful setting for teachers who wish to enhance their own professional development. A self-generated group of teachers—it might call itself Intentional Teachers Anonymous—interested in how and why they do what they do as teachers can provide information, feedback, and emotional support.

Because such professional education activities are self-generated, they are quite different from the experience of a summer university course or an in-service day. A mutual-aid group reflects the teachers' own concerns rather than external requirements. Like users of a learning network, group members determine what is to be learned, how it is being learned, and when it has been learned. In such groups teachers can work on acquiring new skills, a process that is essential for exercising intentionality. They can also discuss when the use of particular skills is appropriate, or what skills and approaches are called for in particular situations.

Each member might identify an intention related to some aspect of the controller, manager, or helper role. One member might intend to increase the rate of positive verbal reinforcement given to pupils. Another might intend to plan more learning experiences that involve nonclassroom activities. A third might intend to increase the number of I-messages sent to learners, clients, or colleagues.

Group discussion of these intentions can deal with questions related to information presented in this chapter. Can persons be identified who already model the intention? What feeling components does the intention include? What consequences are anticipated from exercising the intention? What skills are required in order to actualize the intention?

Once an intention is determined to be clear and appropriate, the group can assist in planning experiences requiring that the intention be expressed in action. They will consider what precisely is the desired behavior. Where and when is it likely to occur? How will it be observed and recorded? What form of feedback to the actor is appropriate? Group members can help to interpret observational data and to aid in possible reformulation of the intention.

As members choose intentions reflecting a particular role, the group is likely to debate the superiority of each role. Does more effective teaching result from the controller role? The manager role? The helper role? Such discussion is likely to be stimulating; it is certain to be inconclusive. Which role is "best" depends on a number of factors—the type of setting, characteristics of the learner, characteristics of the teacher, desired learning outcomes, and so on.

The intentional teacher is not wedded to one role but is master of all these roles and probably of still other roles. The intentional teacher not only possesses the skills to be controller or manager or helper but also must master a "meta-skill" of intentionality, a skill that a mutual-aid group can do much to foster. This meta-skill is the wisdom to choose the role—in both intention and behavior—that is appropriate for the situation at hand.

FOR FURTHER READING

A comprehensive review of the role of intention in theories of motivation is given by Ryan (1970). His book, *Intentional Behavior*, integrates a considerable amount of experimental research and also provides a helpful discussion of the levels of explanation addressed by various approaches to intentions.

A stimulating discussion of *Assumptions about Human Nature* is provided by Wrightsman (1974).

Minicourse materials have been developed by the Far West Laboratory for Educational Research and Development (1855 Folsom Street, San Francisco, California 94103) and are distributed by Macmillan Publishing Company.

REFERENCES

Abt, C. C. *Serious games*. New York: Viking, 1970.

Ackoff, R. L. Toward an idealized university. *Management Science*, 1968, *15*(4), B121–B131.

Adams, D. M. *Simulation games: An approach to learning*. Worthington, Ohio: Jones, 1973.

Adams, R. S., & Biddle, B. J. *Realities of teaching: Explorations with video tape*. New York: Holt, Rinehart & Winston, 1970.

Alschuler, A. S. Teaching achievement motivation. In Aerospace Education Foundation (Ed.), *Technology and innovation in education*. New York: Praeger, 1968. Pp. 29–34.

Alschuler, A. S. *Developing achievement motivation in adolescents*. Englewood Cliffs, N. J.: Educational Technology Publications, 1973.

Alschuler, A. S., & Ivey, A. The human side of competency-based education. *Educational Technology*, 1972, *12*(11), 53–55.

Amidon, E., & Giammatteo, M. The verbal behavior of superior elementary teachers. In E. J. Amidon & J. B. Hough (Eds.), *Interaction analysis: Theory, research and application*. Reading, Mass.: Addison-Wesley, 1967. Pp. 186–188.

Anderson, J., Trilling, H., Moody, R., and Rosen, R. *Dirty water*. Cambridge, Mass.: Urban Systems, Inc., 1970.

Anonymous. *Twelve steps and twelve traditions*. New York: Harper & Brothers, 1953.

Argyris, C. Review of *Beyond Freedom and Dignity*. *Harvard Educational Review*, 1971, *41*, 550–567.

Argyris, C. Dangers in applying results from experimental social psychology. *American Psychologist*, 1975, *30*, 469–485.

Aronson, E. The jigsaw route to learning and liking. *Psychology Today*, 1975, *8*(9), 43–50.

Back, K. W. *Beyond words: The story of sensitivity training and the encounter movement*. Baltimore: Penguin, 1973.

Bassin, A. The therapeutic community teaching concept in behavioral science education. *Teaching of Psychology*, 1974, *1*, 64–68.

Beach, L. R. Self-directed student groups and college learning. *Higher Education*, 1974, *3*, 187–200.

Bebout, J. A study of group encounter in higher education. *Educational Technology*, 1973, *13*(3), 63–67.

Becker, W. C. Applications of behavior principals in typical classrooms. In C. E.

Thoresen (Ed.), *Behavior modification in education* (The seventy-second yearbook of the National Society for the Study of Education). Chicago: University of Chicago Press, 1973. Pp. 77–106.

Becker, W. C., Englemann, S., & Thomas, D. R. *Teaching: Volume I, Classroom management; Volume II, Cognitive learning and instruction.* Chicago: Science Research Associates, 1975.

Beltz, S. E. *How to make Johnny want to obey.* Englewood Cliffs, N. J.: Prentice-Hall, 1971.

Bereiter, C. *Must we educate?* Englewood Cliffs, N. J.: Prentice-Hall, 1973.

Berte, N. R. (Ed.). Individualizing education by learning contracts. *New Directions for Higher Education #10,* 1975, *3*(2).

Blake, R. R., Mouton, J. S., Barnes, L. B., & Greiner, L. E. Breakthrough in organizational development. In R. T. Golembiewski & A. Blumberg (Eds.), *Sensitivity training and the laboratory approach: Readings about concepts and applications.* Itasca, Ill.: Peacock, 1970. Pp. 390–413.

Block, J. H. (Ed.). *Mastery learning: Theory and practice.* New York: Holt, Rinehart & Winston, 1971.

Block, J. H., & Anderson, L. W. *Mastery learning in classroom instruction.* New York: Macmillan, 1975.

Bolstad, O. D., & Johnson, S. M. Self-regulation in the modification of disruptive classroom behavior. *Journal of Applied Behavior Analysis,* 1972, *5,* 443–454.

Borman, L. D. (Ed.). *Explorations in self-help and mutual aid.* Evanston, Ill.: Center for Urban Affairs, Northwestern University, 1975.

Campbell, J. P., & Dunnette, M. D. Effectiveness of T-group experiences in managerial training and development. *Psychological Bulletin,* 1968, *70,* 73–104.

Carkhuff, R. R. *Helping and human relations* (Vols. 1 & 2). New York: Holt, Rinehart & Winston, 1969.

Carroll, J. B. A model of school learning. *Teachers College Record,* 1963, *64,* 723–733.

Coleman, J. R. *Blue-collar journal: A college president's sabbatical.* Philadelphia: Lippincott, 1974.

Coleman, J. S., Livingston, S. A., Fennessey, G. M., Edwards, K. J., & Kidder, S. J. The Hopkins Game Program: Conclusions from seven years of research. *Educational Researcher,* 1973, *2*(8), 3–7.

Coulson, W. R. Inside a basic encounter group. *The Counseling Psychologist,* 1970, *2*(2), 1–27.

Coulson, W. R. *Groups, gimmicks, and instant gurus: An examination of encounter groups and their distortions.* New York: Harper & Row, 1972.

Cox, J. A., & Patton, M. L. A comparison of teachers and tutors in terms of psychological need. *American Psychological Association Experimental Publications System,* 1970, *8,* Ms #278-46.

De Charms, R. From pawns to origins: Toward self-motivation. In G. S. Lesser (Ed.), *Psychology and educational practice.* Glenview, Ill.: Scott, Foresman, 1971. Pp. 380–407.

Drakeford, J. W. *Farewell to the lonely crowd.* Waco, Texas: Word Books, 1969.

Dunn, R., & Dunn, K. *Practical approaches to individualizing instruction: Contracts and other effective teaching strategies.* West Nyack, N.Y.: Parker, 1972.

Egan, G. *Face to face: The small-group experience and interpersonal growth.* Monterey, Calif.: Brooks/Cole, 1973.

Erb, E. D., & Hooker, D. *The psychology of the emerging self: An integrated interpretation of goal-directed behavior.* Philadelphia: Davis, 1967.

Fishbein, M., & Ajzen, I. *Belief, attitude, intention and behavior: An introduction to theory and research.* Reading, Mass.: Addison-Wesley, 1975.

Flanders, N. A. Intent, action, and feedback: A preparation for teaching. *Journal of Teacher Education,* 1963, *14,* 251–260.

Gallup, G. H. Sixth annual Gallup Poll of public attitudes toward education. *Phi Delta Kappan,* 1974, *56,* 20–32.

Gartner, A., Kohler, M. C., & Riessman, F. *Children teach children: Learning by teaching.* New York: Harper & Row, 1971.

Gendlin, E. T. A short summary and some long predictions. In J. T. Hart & T. M. Tomlinson (Eds.), *New directions in client-centered therapy.* Boston: Houghton-Mifflin, 1970. Pp. 544–562.

Gentile, J. R., Frazier, T. W., & Morris, M. C. *Instructional applications of behavioral principles.* Monterey, Calif.: Brooks/Cole, 1975.

Gibbons, M. Walkabout: Searching for the right passage from childhood and school. *Phi. Delta Kappan,* 1974, *55,* 596–602.

Golembiewski, R. T., & Blumberg, A. (Eds.). *Sensitivity training and the laboratory approach: Readings about concepts and applications.* Itasca, Ill.: Peacock, 1970.

Good, T. L., & Brophy, J. E. *Looking in classrooms.* New York: Harper & Row, 1973.

Goodlad, J. I., Klein, M. F., and associates. *Behind the classroom door.* Worthington, Ohio: Jones, 1970.

Gordon, T. *T. E. T.: Teacher effectiveness training.* New York: Wyden, 1974.

Gray, F., Graubard, P. S., & Rosenberg, H. Little brother is changing you. *Psychology Today,* 1974, *7*(10), 42–46.

Greenblat, C. S., & Duke, R. D. *Gaming-simulation: Rationale, design, and applications.* New York: Halsted, 1975.

Gustaitis, R. *Turning on.* New York: Signet, 1969.

Harris, F. R., Johnston, M. K., Kelley, C. S., & Wolf, M. M. Effects of positive social reinforcement on regressed crawling of a nursery school child. *Journal of Educational Psychology,* 1964, *55,* 35–41.

Hart, J. T. A conversation with Carl Rogers. In J. T. Hart & T. M. Tomlinson (Eds.), *New directions in client-centered therapy.* Boston: Houghton-Mifflin, 1970. Pp. 502–534.

Hartman, R. A. H. Volunteerism in the volunteer state. *Phi Delta Kappan,* 1975, *66,* 608–609.

Hendricks, C. G., Thoresen, C. E., & Hubbard, D. R. Effects of behavioral self-observation on elementary teachers and students (Research and Development Memorandum No. 121). Stanford, Calif.: Stanford Center for Research and Development in Teaching, 1974.

Hills, C., & Stone, R. B. *Conduct your own awareness sessions.* New York: Signet, 1970.

Holt, J. *How children fail.* New York: Pitman, 1964.

Homme, L., C'de Baca, P., Cottingham, L., & Homme, A. What behavioral engineering is. *Psychological Record,* 1968, *18,* 425–434.

Homme, L., & Tosti, D. *Behavior technology: Motivation and contingency management.* San Rafael, Calif.: Individual Learning Systems, 1971.

Horn, R. E. *Participative decision-making.* Lexington, Mass.: Information Resources, Inc., 1970.

Houriet, R. *Getting back together.* New York: Coward, McCann & Geoghegan, 1971.

Howard, J. *Please touch: A guided tour of the human potential movement.* New York: McGraw-Hill, 1970.

Hurvitz, N. Peer self-help psychotherapy groups and their implications for psychotherapy. *Psychotherapy: Theory, research and practice,* 1970, *7,* 41–49.

Hurvitz, N. Peer self-help psychotherapy groups: Psychotherapy without psychotherapists. In P. M. Roman & H. M. Trice (Eds.), *The sociology of psychotherapy.* New York: Jason Aronson, 1974. Pp. 84–138.

Illich, I. *Deschooling society.* New York: Harper & Row, 1971.

Ivey, A. E. The intentional individual: A process-outcome view of behavioral psychology. *The Counseling Psychologist,* 1969, *1*(4), 56–60.

Ivey, A. E. *Microcounseling: Innovations in interviewing training.* Springfield, Ill.: Thomas, 1972.

Johnson, D. W., & Johnson, R. T. Instructional goal structure: Cooperative, competitive, or individualistic. *Review of Educational Research,* 1974, *44,* 213–240.

Joyce, B., & Weil, M. *Models of teaching.* Englewood Cliffs, N. J.: Prentice-Hall, 1972.

Katz, A. H., & Bender, E. I. *The strength in us: Self-help groups in the modern world.* New York: Franklin Watts, 1976.

Katz, R. A solo-survival experience as education for personal growth. *Educational Opportunity Forum,* 1969, *1*(4), 38–53.

Kazdin, A. E. Self-monitoring and behavior change. In M. J. Mahoney & C. E. Thoresen (Eds.), *Self-control: Power to the person.* Monterey, Calif.: Brooks/Cole, 1974. Pp. 218–246.

Keller, F. S. "Good-bye teacher . . ." *Journal of Applied Behavior Analysis,* 1968, *1,* 79–89.

Kinkade, K. *A Walden Two experiment: The first five years of Twin Oaks Community.* New York: William Morrow, 1973.

Klaus, D. J. Patterns of peer tutoring. Paper presented at the meeting of the American Educational Research Association, Washington, D. C., March 1975.

Kolesnik, W. B. *Humanism and/or behaviorism in education.* Boston: Allyn & Bacon, 1975.

Kozol, J. *Death at an early age.* New York: Bantam, 1968.

Kulik, J. A., Kulik, C. L., & Carmichael, K. The Keller Plan in science teaching. *Science,* 1974, *183,* 379–383.

Lakin, M. *Experiential groups: The uses of interpersonal encounter, psychotherapy groups, and sensitivity training.* Morristown, N. J.: General Learning Press, 1972.

Levine, F. M., & Fasnacht, F. Token rewards may lead to token learning. *American Psychologist,* 1974, *29,* 816–820.

Lewis, H. R., & Streitfeld, H. S. *Growth games: How to tune in yourself, your family, your friends.* New York: Bantam, 1972.

Lieberman, M. A., Yalom, I. D., & Miles, M. B. *Encounter groups: First facts.* New York: Basic, 1973.

Madsen, C. H., Jr., & Madsen, C. K. *Teaching/discipline: A positive approach for educational development* (2nd ed.). Boston: Allyn & Bacon, 1974.

Maehr, M. L. *Sociocultural origins of achievement.* Monterey, Calif.: Brooks/Cole, 1974.

Mager, R. F. *Preparing instructional objectives.* Palo Alto, Calif.: Fearon, 1962.

Mahoney, M. J., & Thoresen, C. E. *Self-control: Power to the person.* Monterey, Calif.: Brooks/Cole, 1974.

Mann, J. *Encounter: A weekend with intimate strangers.* New York: Pocket, 1971.

Matson, F. W. (Ed.). *Without/within: Behaviorism and humanism.* Monterey, Calif.: Brooks/Cole, 1973.

May, R. *Love and will.* New York: Norton, 1969.

McGaghie, W. C., & Menges, R. J. Assessing self-directed learning. *Teaching of Psychology,* 1975, *2,* 56–59.

McGaghie, W. C., Menges, R. J., & Dobroski, B. J. Self-modification in a college course: Outcomes and correlates. *Journal of Counseling Psychology,* 1976, *23,* 178–182.

McNall, S. G. Peer teaching: A description and evaluation. *Teaching Sociology,* 1975, *2,* 133–146.

Meichenbaum, D., & Cameron, R. The clinical potential of modifying what clients say to themselves. In M. J. Mahoney & C. E. Thoresen (Eds.), *Self-control: Power to the person.* Monterey, Calif.: Brooks/Cole, 1974. Pp. 263–290.

Melaragno, R. J. *Tutoring with students.* Englewood Cliffs, N. J.: Educational Technology Publications, 1976.

Menges, R. J. Freedom to learn: Self-directed study in a required course. *Journal of Teacher Education,* 1972, *23,* 32–39.

Menges, R. J., & McGaghie, W. C. Learning in group settings: Toward a classification of outcomes. *Educational Technology,* 1974, *14,* 56–60.

Menges, R. J., & Pennington, F. *A survey of nineteen innovative educational programs for adolescents and adults.* Minneapolis, Minn.: Youth Research Center, 1971.

Mosston, M. *Teaching: From command to discovery.* Belmont, Calif.: Wadsworth, 1972.

Mowrer, O. H. Integrity groups: Principles and procedures. *The Counseling Psychologist,* 1972, *3*(2), 7–33.

Napier, R., Hayman, J., & Moskowitz, G. *Classroom dynamics: Viewing the classroom as a social system.* Monterey, Calif.: Brooks/Cole, 1976.

National Training Laboratories Institute. *NTL 1975 Summer Programs.* Arlington, Va.: NTL Institute, 1975.

Nidetch, J. *The story of Weight Watchers.* New York: W/W Twenty-first Corp. (Distributed by New American Library), 1970.

Nolan, J. D. The true humanist: The behavior modifier. *Teachers College Record,* 1974, *76,* 335–343.

O'Banion, T., & O'Connell, A. *The shared journey: An introduction to encounter.* Englewood Cliffs, N. J.: Prentice-Hall, 1970.

Parloff, M. B. Group therapy and the small group field: An encounter. *International Journal of Group Psychotherapy,* 1970, *20,* 267–304.

Phenix, P. H. *Realms of meaning: A philosophy of the curriculum for general education.* New York: McGraw-Hill, 1964.

Powell, B. S. Children as teachers: Stages in cross age tutoring. Paper presented at the meeting of the American Educational Research Association, Washington, D. C., March 1975.

Resources for Youth. Internships. *Resources for Youth Newsletter,* 1975, *5*(2), 1.

Richmond, G. *The micro-society school: A real world in miniature.* New York: Harper & Row, 1973.

Roberts, R. E. *The new communes: Coming together in America.* Englewood Cliffs, N. J.: Prentice-Hall, 1971.

Rogers, C. R. *Client-centered therapy.* Boston: Houghton-Mifflin, 1951.

Rogers, C. R. *Carl Rogers on encounter groups.* New York: Harper & Row, 1970.

Rogers, J. Using behavioral objectives menus in the survey course. *Educational Technology,* 1972, *12*(8), 17–19.

Ruitenbeek, H. M. *The new group therapies.* New York: Avon, 1970.

Ruskin, R. S. *The personalized system of instruction: An educational alternative.* Washington, D. C.: The American Association for Higher Education, 1974.

Russell, E. W. The power of behavior control: A critique of behavior modification methods. *Journal of Clinical Psychology,* 1974, *30,* 111–136.

Ryan, B. A. *PSI. Keller's personalized system of instruction: An appraisal.* Washington, D. C.: American Psychological Association, 1974.

Ryan, T. A. *Intentional behavior: An approach to human motivation.* New York: Ronald Press, 1970.

Sagarin, E. *Odd man in: Societies of deviants in America.* Chicago: Quadrangle, 1969.

Sax, S., & Hollander, S. *Reality games.* New York: Macmillan, 1972.

Shapiro, S. B. Some aspects of a theory of interpersonal contracts. *Psychological Reports,* 1968, *22,* 171–183.

Shepard, M., & Lee, M. *Marathon 16.* New York: Pocket, 1971.

Shukraft, R., & Washburn, J. *Impact: A youth ministry simulation.* San Francisco: San Francisco Theological Seminary, 1970.

Skinner, B. F. *Walden two.* New York: Macmillan, 1948.

Skinner, B. F. *The technology of teaching.* New York: Appleton-Century-Crofts, 1968.

Skinner, B. F. *Contingencies of reinforcement: A theoretical analysis.* New York: Appleton-Century-Crofts, 1969.(a)

Skinner, B. F. Contingency management in the classroom. *Education,* 1969, *90* 93–100. (b)

Skinner, B. F. *Beyond freedom and dignity.* New York: Knopf, 1971.

Skinner, B. F. *About behaviorism.* New York: Knopf, 1974.

Smith, P. B. Controlled studies of the outcome of sensitivity training. *Psychological Bulletin,* 1975, *82,* 597–622.

Sohl, J. *The lemon eaters.* New York: Dell, 1968.

Stadsklev, R. (Ed.). *Handbook of simulation gaming in social education* (Part 1, Textbook; Part 2, Directory). University, Alabama: University of Alabama Institute of Higher Education Research and Services, 1974–1975.

Tharp, R. G., Watson, D., & Kaya, J. Self-modification of depression. *Journal of Consulting and Clinical Psychology,* 1974, *42,* 624.

Thompson, M., Brassell, W. R., Persons, S., Tucker, R., & Rollins, H. Contingency management in the schools: How often and how well does it work? *American Educational Research Journal,* 1974, *11,* 19–28.

Thoresen, C. E. (Ed.). *Behavior modification in education* (The seventy-second yearbook of the National Society for the Study of Education). Chicago: University of Chicago Press, 1973.

Thoresen, C. E., & Coates, T. J. Behavioral self-control: Some clinical concerns. In M. Hersen, R. M. Eisler, & P. M. Miller (Eds.), *Progress in behavior modification* (Vol. 2). New York: Academic Press, 1976.

Traunstein, D. M., & Steinman, R. Voluntary self-help organizations: An exploratory study. *Journal of Voluntary Action Research,* 1973, *4,* 230–239.

Ulrich, R., Stachnik, T., & Mabry, J. *Control of human behavior, Vol. III, Behavior modification in education.* Glenview, Ill.: Scott Foresman, 1974.

Von Haden, H. I., & King, J. M. *Educational innovator's guide.* Worthington, Ohio: Jones, 1974.

Wardrop, J. L. *Standardized testing in the schools: Uses and roles.* Monterey, Calif.: Brooks/Cole, 1975.

Watson, D., & Tharp, R. *Self-directed behavior: Self-modification for personal adjustment.* Monterey, Calif.: Brooks/Cole, 1972.

Wentworth, D. R., & Lewis, D. R. A review of research on instructional games and simulations in social studies education. *Social Education,* 1973, *37,* 432–440.

Werner, T., & McLaughlin, D. Kiddie PSI. *PSI Newsletter,* 1975, *3*(3), 1–6.

White, M. A. Natural rates of teacher approval and disapproval in the classroom. *Journal of Applied Behavior Analysis,* 1975, *8,* 367–372.

Wick, J. W. *Educational measurement: Where are we going and how will we know when we get there?* Columbus, Ohio: Merrill, 1973.

Wildman, R. W. II, & Wildman, R. W. The generalization of behavior modification procedures: A review with special emphasis on classroom applications. *Psychology in the Schools,* 1975, *12,* 432–445.

Williams, R. L., & Long, J. D. *Toward a self-managed life style.* Boston: Houghton-Mifflin, 1975.

Willower, D. J., Eidell, T. L., & Hoy, W. K. *The school and pupil control ideology.* University Park, Penn.: Pennsylvania State University Studies, No. 24, 1973.

Wittmer, J., & Myrick, R. D. *Facilitative teaching: Theory and practice.* Pacific Palisades, Calif.: Goodyear, 1974.

Wrightsman, L. S. *Assumptions about human nature: A social-psychological perspective.* Monterey, Calif.: Brooks/Cole, 1974.

Yablonsky, L. *The tunnel back: Synanon.* New York: Macmillan, 1965.

Zuckerman, D. W., & Horn, R. E. *The guide to simulations/games for education and training.* Lexington, Mass.: Information-Resources, Inc., 1973.

AUTHOR INDEX

Abt, C. C., 59
Ackoff, R. L., 51, 52
Adams, D. M., 59
Adams, R. S., 63
Ajzen, I., 100, 101, 102
Alschuler, A. S., 79, 94, 103
Amidon, E., 63
Anderson, J., 42
Anderson, L. W., 37, 58
Argyris, C., 19, 31
Aronson, E., 50

Back, K. W., 94
Bassin, A., 95
Beach, L. R., 59
Bebout, J., 80
Becker, W. C., 14, 32
Beltz, S. E., 19
Bender, E. I., 94
Bereiter, C., 20
Berte, N. R., 58
Biddle, B. J., 63
Blake, R., 78
Block, J. H., 34, 37, 58
Blumberg, A., 76
Bolstad, O. D., 31
Borman, L. D., 86
Brassell, W. R., 17
Brophy, J. E., 51, 98

Cameron, R., 26
Campbell, J. P., 81
Carkhuff, R. R., 65
Carmichael, K., 37
Carroll, J. B., 37
Coates, T. J., 32
Coleman, J. R., 44, 45, 48
Coleman, J. S., 43, 44

Coulson, W. R., 62, 72, 74, 82
Cox, J. A., 51

De Charms, R., 94
Dederich, C., 92
Descartes, 100
Detzel, D., 54
Dobroski, B. J., 27
Drakeford, J. W., 90, 94
Duke, R. D., 59
Dunn, K., 40, 57, 58
Dunn, R., 40, 57, 58
Dunnette, M. D., 81

Egan, G., 94
Eidell, T. L., 6
Englemann, S., 32
Erb, E. D., 65

Fasnacht, F., 21
Fishbein, M., 100, 101, 102
Flanders, N. A., 62
Frazier, T. W., 32

Gallup, G. H., 5
Gartner, A., 59
Gendlin, E. T., 70
Gentile, J. R., 32
Giammatteo, M., 63
Gibbons, M., 59
Golembiewski, R. T., 76
Good, T. L., 51, 98
Goodlad, J. I., 62
Gordon, T., 66
Graubard, P. S., 31
Gray, R., 31
Greenblat, C. S., 59
Gustaitis, R., 83, 88, 94

Harris, F. R., 10
Hart, J. T., 81
Hartman, R. A. H., 51
Hayman, J., 94, 95
Hendricks, C. G., 27
Hills, C., 76
Hollander, S., 94
Holt, J., 31
Homme, L., 9, 32
Hooker, D., 65
Horn, R. E., 41, 42, 59
Houriet, R., 11
Howard, J., 78, 94
Hoy, W. K., 6
Hubbard, D. R., 27
Hurvitz, N., 91, 92, 94

Illich, I., 54
Ivey, A. E., 103, 104

Johnson, D. W., 59
Johnson, R. T., 59
Johnson, S. M., 31
Johnston, M. K., 10
Joyce, B., 105

Katz, A. H., 94
Katz, R., 48
Kaya, J., 25
Kazdin, A. E., 27
Keller, F. S., 35, 37, 58
Kelley, C. S., 10
King, J. M., 57
Kinkade, K., 32
Klaus, D. J., 52
Kohler, M. C., 59
Kolesnik, W. B., 32
Kozol, J., 31
Kulik, C. L., 37
Kulik, J. A., 37

Lakin, M., 74
Larson, R., 66
Lee, M., 76
Levine, F. M., 21
Lewis, D. R., 44
Lewis, H. R., 94
Lewis, R., 54
Lieberman, M. A., 80
Long, J. D., 32

Mabry, J., 19
Madsen, C. H., Jr., 6, 32, 98
Madsen, C. K., 6, 32, 98
Maehr, M., 94
Mager, R. F., 58
Mahoney, M. J., 32, 103
Mann, J., 76
Matson, F. W., 32
May, R., 99, 100
McGaghie, W., 24, 27, 70, 94
McLaughlin, D., 35
McNall, S. G., 59
Meichenbaum, D., 26
Melaragno, R. J., 59
Menges, R. J., 24, 27, 40, 70, 92, 94
Miles, M. B., 80
Moreno, J., 72
Morris, M. C., 32
Moskowitz, G., 94, 95
Mosston, M., 33, 34, 50, 57
Mowrer, O. H., 89, 90
Myrick, R. D., 69

Napier, R., 94, 95
Nidetch, J., 89, 90
Nolan, J. D., 13, 15

O'Banion, T., 94
O'Connell, A., 94

Parloff, M. B., 82
Patton, M. L., 51
Pennington, F., 92
Persons, S., 17
Phenix, P. H., 71
Powell, B. S., 51

Richmond, G., 58
Riessman, F., 59
Roberts, R. E., 12
Rogers, C. R., 65, 66, 72, 73, 81, 82, 83, 94
Rogers, J., 39
Rollins, H., 17
Rosenberg, H., 31
Ruitenbeek, H. M., 72, 74
Ruskin, R. S., 58
Russell, E. W., 20, 21, 22
Ryan, B. A., 58
Ryan, T. A., 109

Sagarin, E., 86, 94
Sax, S., 94
Shapiro, S. B., 39
Shepard, M., 76
Shukraft, R., 42
Skinner, B. F., 6, 7, 8, 10, 11, 12, 18, 19, 20, 32
Smith, P. B., 81
Sohl, J., 76
Stachnik, T., 19
Stadsklev, R., 59
Steinman, R., 86
Stone, R. B., 76
Streitfeld, H. S., 94

Tharp, R. G., 23, 25, 32
Thomas, D. R., 32
Thompson, M., 17, 22
Thoresen, C. E., 16, 27, 32, 103
Tosti, D., 32
Traunstein, D. M., 86
Tucker, R., 17

Ulrich, R., 19

Von Haden, H. I., 57

Wardrop, J. L., 57
Washburn, J., 42
Watson, D., 23, 25, 32
Weil, M., 105
Wentworth, D. R., 44
Werner, T., 35
White, M. A., 6
Wick, J. W., 58
Wildman, R. W., 21
Wildman, R. W., II, 21
Williams, D., 66
Williams, R. L., 32
Willower, D. J., 6
Wittmer, J., 69
Wolf, M. M., 10
Wrightsman, L. S., 110

Yablonsky, L., 88
Yalom, I. D., 80

Zuckerman, D. W., 41, 59

SUBJECT INDEX

Achievement-motivation training, 79, 80

Alcoholics Anonymous, 63, 83–87, 91

Basic Human Interaction Laboratory, 77

Behavior modification (*see* Behavioral psychology)

Behavior therapy, 22, 23

Behavioral psychology
 claims for, 13–15
 control of antecedents, 8, 9, 16, 18, 19, 28
 control of consequences, 9, 10, 16, 18, 19, 28
 description of, 7, 8
 and intention, 102–104
 objections to, 17–22
 and psychotherapy, 22
 and research, 15–17, 26–28
 and self-modification of behavior, 22–26, 28–30
 teachers trained in, 30, 31
 at Twin Oaks, 11–13

Cognitive learning
 and encounter groups, 71, 80
 and expression of feelings, 94
 through tutoring, 52

Contracts (*see* Teacher-learner contracts)

Corporal punishment (*see* Discipline)

"Democracy" (learning simulation), 41

Determinism and freedom, 99

Discipline
 and behavioral psychology, 8, 9, 12–17, 30, 31
 and corporal punishment, 6
 public attitudes about, 5
 traditional views of, 6, 7

Emotions
 empathy, 64, 65, 69, 93
 expression of, 39
 I-messages, 66–69, 93
 and groups, 70–76
 and schools, 61–63, 70, 93
 and teachers, 57, 106

Encounter groups, 63, 72–76, 80, 81, 94

Evaluation
 and behavioral psychology, 21
 by learner, 38, 39, 40, 44, 49, 50, 80
 and mastery learning, 35, 37
 by teachers, 33, 34, 53, 62
 by tutors, 50, 53

Experiential learning
 nature of, 43
 total immersion, 46–48

Experimental analysis of behavior (*see* Behavioral psychology)

Far West Laboratory for Educational Research and Development, 110

Gallup International
 polls about public schools, 5

Games and simulations, 41–44, 58

Grades (*see* Evaluation)

Grid Seminars, 78, 81, 82
Groups (*see* Encounter groups, Mutual-aid and self-help groups)

I-messages, 66–69, 77, 93, 109
Integrity Groups, 89–92
Intention
  and congruence with behavior, 105
  defined, 97
  developing clarity of, 105–108
  and discrepancy with behavior, 3, 97, 98, 100, 106, 107
  and group support for actualizing, 108, 109
  "minicourse" materials for, 106
  three approaches to, 99–107
  theory and research, 96, 98
Intentional teachers, 3, 4, 109
Intentional Teachers Anonymous, 108
Internship training, 46

"Jabberwockey" (learning simulation), 42

Learners
  as decision makers, 23, 34, 44
  as teachers, 49–53, 56, 59
Learning
  behavioral approach to, 7, 8, 10
  controlled by learners, 53, 54
  and emotions, 61, 62
  individual rates of, 37, 38
  from personal experience, 39, 43–49, 71
  (*see also* Evaluation)
Learning Exchange, The, 53, 54, 60
Learning Networks, 53–57, 108

Managerial Grid, 78
Mastery learning, 34–38, 43, 56, 58
Mutual-aid and self-help groups, 83–94, 108, 109

National Training Laboratories, 77, 81, 94
National Training School for Boys, 10

Objectives (*see* Teacher-learner contracts)
Outward Bound Schools, 47, 48, 59

Personalized System of Instruction, 35, 36, 58
Psychotherapy
  and behavioral principles, 22, 23
Punishment of students (*see* Discipline)

Reinforcement
  in mastery learning, 35–37
  negative, 12, 13, 52, 103
  positive, 12–17, 21, 22, 50, 52, 104, 108
  in self-modification projects, 23–26
Resources for Youth, 46

Scientific Methods, Inc., 78
Self-modification (*see* Behavioral psychology)
"SIMSOC, Simulated Society" (learning simulation), 41
Social psychology
  and intention, 100–102
Standardized tests, 57
Student behavior (*see* Discipline)
Synanon, 87, 88, 90, 91, 92
Synnoetics, 71

Teacher Effectiveness Training, 66, 77
Teacher-learner contracts, 38–41, 58
Teachers
  as controllers, 1, 2, 5–32, 105
  and emotions, 57, 63, 93, 105, 106
  as helpers, 1, 2, 3, 61–95, 105
  and helping skills, 93, 106
  and intention, 96, 98
  as managers, 1–3, 33–59, 105
  training in behavioral principles, 30
  use of punishment, 6
  and verbal domination, 62, 63
T-groups (*see* Training groups)
Total immersion, 41, 44–48, 59
Training groups (T-groups), 63, 76–82, 94

Tutoring, 34, 35, 49–53, 56, 59
Twin Oaks, 11–13

Urban Training Center, 46, 47

Verbal behavior in classrooms, 62, 63

Weight Watchers, 85, 86, 89, 90, 91, 93